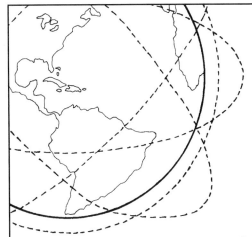

Best Web Sites for Kids 2000

Written by Jessica H. G. Schroeter, M.A., M.L.I.S.

Illustrations by Denice Adorno

 Teacher Created Materials, Inc.

www.teachercreated.com

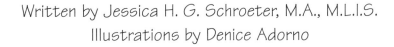

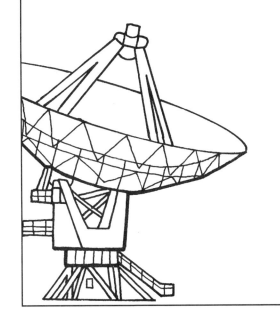

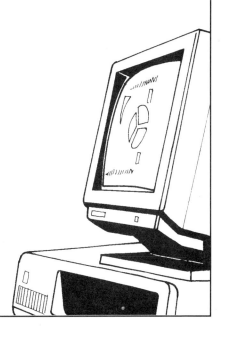

Teacher Created Materials, Inc.

6421 Industry Way

Westminster, CA 92683

©2000 Teacher Created Materials, Inc.

www.teachercreated.com

URL updates available at our Web site

http://www.teachercreated.com/updates/index.html

Reprinted, 2000 b

Made in U.S.A.

Library of Congress Catalog Card Number: 99-64488

ISBN-1-57690-000-2

Editor:

Lynn C. Gustafson, Ed.D.

Table of Contents

So Many Places To Go!

The World Wide Web (WWW) is a wonderful resource for children. It can be compared to a gigantic library containing information on almost every imaginable topic. But unlike a library with books arranged according to clearly defined categories, the ever-expanding number of sites appearing daily on the Internet can be overwhelming and seem to have no organization whatsoever. The Internet does not discriminate between sites created by professionals and non-professionals or by educators and advertisers. Locating Web sites that are educational and enjoyable for an appropriate age level can be extremely time consuming. Parents and teachers are also concerned about sending their children to computers unsupervised. So now that more and more people have access to the Internet from their homes and schools, they are asking themselves the question: "Now that I am connected to the Internet, what should I do with it?"

This book attempts to answer this question by offering a clear and concise collection of some of the most intriguing children's sites for available on the Web today. Highly recommended sites are arranged in a variety of interesting sections. For example, a useful category like "Find That Fact!" offers numerous research Web sites, and the chapter "Kiddie Korner" presents a sampling of sites for the very young Web surfer. You can visit the recommended sites in this book or use them as starting points for your own explorations. Don't fret about spending hours locating appropriate Web sites for kids. All the sites in this book

have been reviewed and are safe, informative, and often very entertaining.

Best Web Sites for Kids 2000 launches you on the Information Superhighway for the 21st Century. Use this book as a guide, and as you flip through the pages, take the opportunity to discover some of the best sites on the Internet for kids. Visit zoos, museums, and travel the world, but most of all, have lots of fun on your explorations!

Who Can Use This Book?

Whether you are a teacher or parent searching for information for school projects or a child looking for fun activities on the computer, this book is for you! To get started, all you need is the following:

- A computer
- Access to the Internet with a modem or cable
- An Internet service provider (ISP)
- Basic experience using search engines
- A desire for advice about Web sites to visit.

If you fit this description, or even if you already have a lot of surfing experience, you will enjoy **Best Web Sites for Kids 2000**. Use this book to find and explore new places in Cyberspace, but don't allow your explorations to end there. Once you have visited and enjoyed all the sites described in this book, follow the many recommended links provided within the Web sites listed in this book and become confident navigating the World Wide Web, where time, space, and location seem to disappear!

Managing Web Resources: Bookmarks

Millions of Web sites are available on the Internet, and it is impossible to remember the lengthy URLs (addresses) associated with all your favorite spots. Since you will undoubtedly want to revisit useful locations again and again, you will need to create a system of organization for your Internet explorations.

That is when bookmarks come into the picture. An electronic bookmark (also called the Favorites List) does the same thing a regular bookmark does: it marks your place. No matter what the feature is called, all current browsers make it possible to "bookmark" a location on the Web for future use. By selecting **Add Bookmark** from the Bookmark menu, the title of a Web page is added to the bottom of your bookmarks list, allowing you to return to the same Web page over and over again.

However, a long list of bookmarks can soon become unmanageable. Often a list grows so long that it seems you are scrolling on and on, making it difficult to find your favorite places on the Internet. Fortunately, browsers contain editing features that make it easy to keep track of the wonderful tools available on the Internet.

The following pages contain directions for using this bookmark feature with *Netscape Communicator* (previously called *Navigator*) and *Internet Explorer.*

Netscape Bookmark Feature

To Create a Bookmark

1. Open **Netscape**.
2. Go to the Web site you want to save.
3. Click on the **Bookmarks** menu on the Location toolbar.
4. Select **Add Bookmark**.
5. Click on the **Bookmarks** menu again to make sure the site has been saved.

After awhile, your list of bookmarks will increase. Add order to it by grouping the bookmarks into folders according to topics. For example, you may organize folders for games, animals, or online dictionaries depending on your interests.

To Organize your Bookmarks (Folders)

1. Find the **Bookmarks** or **Edit Bookmarks** command. In earlier versions of **Navigator** this is found under the **Navigator** icon. In later versions, it is found under the **Bookmarks** menu.
2. Go to the **File** menu and click on **New Folder**.
3. Type in the name of the new folder in the **Name** box.
4. Click **OK** when finished.

Managing Web Resources: Bookmarks *(cont.)*

To Put Bookmarks in a Folder

1. Highlight the bookmark you want to move.

2. Hold down the left mouse button and drag the item (the Web site name) over to the folder.

3. Drop the item into the folder by releasing the mouse button.

To Delete Bookmarks

1. Highlight a bookmark.

2. Press the Delete key.

To Edit Bookmarks

1. Highlight the bookmark.

2. Go to the **Edit** Menu.

3. Select **Get Info**.

4. Change the name or alter the URL at this window.

5. Click **OK**.

To further organize each folder, you can create folders within folders. For example, you may want to create in a science folder subcategories for weather, planets, ecology, and so forth.

To Create a Subfolder

1. Go to the **Bookmark** menu and select **Edit Bookmarks**.

2. Click on the Bookmark folder to which you want to add a subfolder.

3. Either click the arrow or double-click the folder to open it.

4. Go to the **File** menu and select **New Folder**.

5. Type a name in the **Name** box.

6. Click **OK** when finished.

7. Click and drag appropriate bookmarks into the new folder.

8. When you open the main folder, you will see your subfolder beneath it.

Managing Web Resources: Favorites

Internet Explorer Favorite Feature

To Create a Favorite

1. Open **Microsoft Internet Explorer**.

2. Go to the Web site you want to save.

3. Click on the **Favorites** menu on the location toolbar.

4. Select **Add Page to Favorites**.

5. Click on the **Favorites** menu to make sure the Web site has been saved.

To Organize Your Favorites (Folders)

1. Click on Favorites.

2. Select **Organize Favorites**, and a list of your favorites will appear.

3. Go to the **Favorites** menu and select **New Folder**.

4. A folder will appear. Type the title of the folder in the box.

5. Press **Return**.

To Put Favorites in a Folder

1. Highlight the favorites you want to move.

2. Hold down the left mouse button and drag the item (the Web site) over to the folder.

3. Drop the item into the folder by releasing the mouse button.

To Delete Favorites

1. Highlight the favorite.

2. Press the **Delete** key.

To Edit Favorites

1. Go to the **Favorites** menu and select **Organize Favorites**.

2. Highlight the favorites you want to edit.

3. Go to the **File** menu and select **Get Info**.

4. Change the name or alter the URL at this window.

5. Press **OK**.

To Create a Subfolder

1. Click on **Favorites.**

2. Select **Organize Favorites**, and a list of your favorites will appear.

3. Go to the **Favorites** menu and select **New Folder**.

4. A folder will appear. Type the title of the folder in the box.

5. Press **Return**.

6. Highlight the new folder.

7. Hold down the left mouse button and drag the new folder into the main folder.

Plug-Ins

Do you really need plug-ins? The answer to this question is definitely yes! Even if you are using a state-of-the-art browser, technology is still changing at an unprecedented rate. This means that *Netscape Communicator (Navigator is an earlier version)* and *Microsoft Internet Explorer* cannot handle all types of files found on the Internet.

This is why plug-ins are essential for optimal interactions with Web sites. You can think of plug-ins as helpers that aid in displaying files the browser cannot accommodate on its own. For example, audio files, video clips, and animations can't be viewed by your browser alone. Without plug-ins, you will not be able to experience the array of variety found on the Internet.

Fortunately for the World Wide Web user, it is easy to find and download these applications to your computer. Listed on this page are suggested plug-ins along with their Internet addresses. Again, it is highly recommended that you install them before you plunge into the multitude of sites in this book.

One word of caution: There may be costs associated with these downloads so be sure to read the information carefully at each Web site.

Name: *Adobe Acrobat Reader*

Function: Allows you to read electronic documents

URL: http://www.adobe.com/

Name: *Macromedia Shockwave*

Function: Allows you to view interactive content like games and animations

URL: http://www.macromedia.com

Name: *Real Audio*

Function: Allows you to listen to sound on the Internet (This application lets you listen to radio broadcasts over the Internet)

URL: http://www.realaudio.com

The plug-ins mentioned above are suggestions. Keep your eyes open for future developments and additions to this basic list!

Ancient & Medieval Times

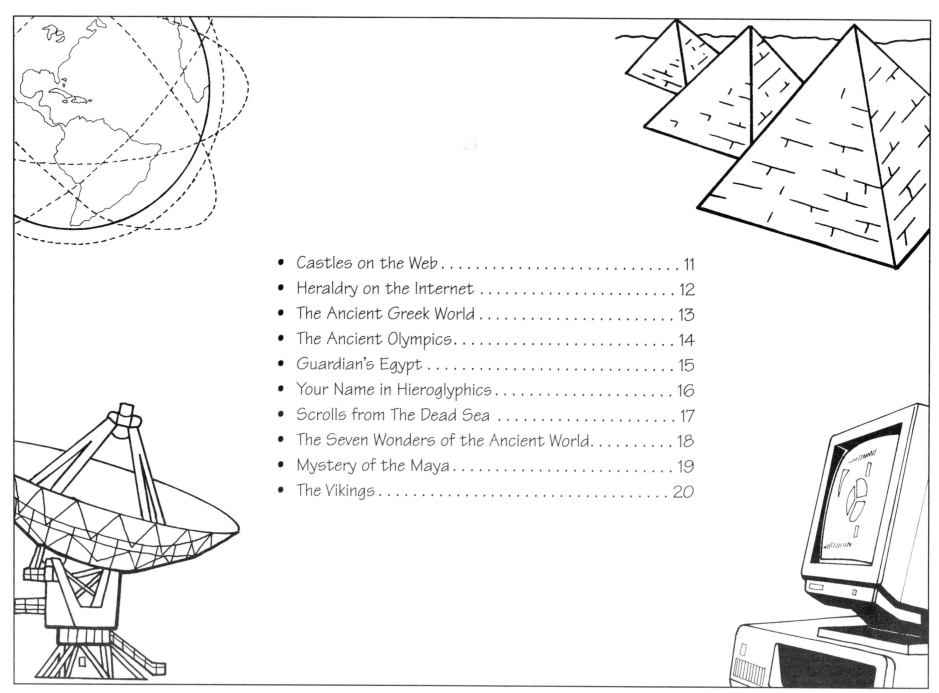

http://www.castlesontheweb.com/

Overview:

Do you like books about King Arthur and Sir Lancelot? If you do, enter the wondrous world of *Castles on the Web*. This comprehensive site organizes the many online resources about medieval castles. If you are interested in heraldry, chivalry, and castle adventures, this is the perfect site for you. Try these sections:

- Castle Tours
- Abbeys and Churches
- Myths and Legends
- Weapons and Supplies
- Castle Greetings

A special section called *Castles for Kids* offers sites with kids' interests in mind. Some places to visit:

- Journey Through the Middle Ages
- Life in the Middle Ages
- Castle Builder

Go back to the time of imposing castles, monarchy, feudalism, and knighthood as you discover the wealth of activities available at this site.

Try this:

Are you reading a Brian Jacques book and need a photograph for a HyperStudio project? Use this site to collect fabulous graphics of medieval imagery.

Highlights:

This site is clearly designed and well organized.

A glossary and links are included.

See also:

The Official Redwall Page

http://www.redwall.org/

Heraldry on the Internet

http://digiserve.com/heraldry/

Overview:

This informative site is designed to help you find heraldry on the Internet. Heraldry appeared during the Middle Ages when people wore armor to protect their faces. This made it impossible to recognize the person behind the armor. So to easily and quickly identify a person or group of people, different coats of arms with specific colors, crests, and symbols were used.

Look for a family name coat of arms used by someone who has the same surname (last name) as you. Search for coats of arms of cities and towns or use *Pimbley's Dictionary of Heraldry* to identify symbols found on coats of arms. The section on clip art contains hundreds of images and a few blank shields so that you can create your own personal coat of arms.

The site is divided into the following sections:

- What's Hot
- Reference
- Heraldry
- Coats of Arms
- Heraldry Articles

- -

Try this:

Click on *Surnames* in the Reference section. Search for your last name and see if there is a coat of arms listed for your family. To create your own, go to the *Clip Art* link under Heraldry.

Highlights:

Teachers would benefit greatly by incorporating this site into a Middle Ages unit.

You will find everything you always wanted to know about heraldry at this site.

See also:

Middle Age Art Exhibit

http://www.learner.org/exhibits/middle ages/

The Ancient Greek World

http://www.museum.upenn.edu/Greek_World/Intro.html

Overview:

Welcome to the online exhibit of The Ancient Greek World presented by the University of Pennsylvania Museum of Archaeology and Anthropology. This site offers artifacts from the museum's permanent collection that provide a backdrop for a vivid story of real life in Ancient Greece.

The site is divided into four thematic units:

- Land and Time—Visit Hellenistic, Classical, Archaic, and other time periods.
- Daily Life—Visit a Greek house and read about fashion.
- Economy—Check out Greek coins, pottery, and cosmetics.
- Religions and Death—Learn about Greek heroes or visit a cemetery.

Try this:

Look at artifacts in the *Geometric Period* (Land and Time). Create your own original work of art using the geometric style.

Highlights:

This is a good starting point for learning about Ancient Greece.

Photographs of artifacts are excellent.

See also:

Mythweb

http://www.mythweb.com/

This site is devoted to heroes, gods, and monsters of Greek mythology.

The Forum of Trajan in Rome: A Virtual Tour

http://www.artsednet.getty.edu/Arts EdNet/Browsing/Trajan/index.html

© Perseus Project

The Ancient Olympics

http://www.perseus.tufts.edu/Olympics/

Overview:

Discus, Chariot racing, Wrestling, and running were all part of the ancient Olympic Games. But which of these events remain part of today's Olympics, the world's largest pageant of athletic skill and international competition? You will find answers to these questions and others at this informative site about the Ancient Olympic Games.

Note: Shockwave plug-ins are required at this site.

Try this:

Go to Athletes' Stories and read about Milo of Kroton, the famous six-time Olympics victor. According to ancient sources, how did Milo show off his strength?

Highlights:

A comprehensive overview of ancient games is provided.

Try the slide show of Olympia; it takes a few minutes to download, but it's worth it!

See also:

The Real Story of Ancient Olympic Games

http://www.upenn.edu/museum/Olympics/olympicintro.html

copyright © 1995-1999 Andrew Bayuk

http://guardians.net/egypt

Overview:

Welcome to Guardian's Egypt, a site where you can explore the mystery and splendor of Ancient Egypt! Find articles, pictures, essays, songs, games, and facts about everything Egyptian. Start by touring some of the sophisticated monuments at the *Great Pyramid* link. Once arriving there, take a virtual tour through its ancient chambers and tunnels. Then visit the *Mummies*, go on a *Cool Dig*, visit Egyptian Museums, and find information about Kings and Pharaohs.

An exciting part of this site is the *Guardian's Cyberjourney*. Enjoy photographs of tombs, temples, antiquities, and more at this fascinating section.

Try this:

Particularly worth visiting is the *Ancient Egypt Kid Connection*. Try *Make Your Own Mummy*, *The Pyramid Crossword Puzzle*, or *Design and Make an Ancient Egyptian Box*.

Visit the Little Horus Web site designed for children to explore Egypt in English or Arabic.

Highlights:

From pyramids to mummies, hieroglyphs to pharaohs, this site is packed with information, links, photographs, and interactive activities.

See also:

The Rosetta Stone Exhibit at the Cleveland Museum of Art

http://www.clemusart.com/archive/pharaoh/rosetta/

Mysteries of Egypt

http://www.civilization.ca/membrs/civiliz/egypt/egypt_e.html

Your Name in Hieroglyphics

http://www.iut.univ-paris8.fr/~rosmord/nomhiero.html

Overview:

Enter this site created by Serge Rosmorduc and have your name transformed into hieroglyphics, an ancient Egyptian language from 3,000 years ago! Don't be concerned when you see the title "Nom en Hieroglyphes" in French on your computer monitor! You have arrived at the correct destination and if you read on, you will notice that English is also used to explain how to use this site.

This site, while visually unimpressive, is actually widely accessed and lots of fun. To use this page, write your name phonetically in the space provided, and then click on *Send*. Wait about 10 seconds, and you will see your name in hieroglyphics.

Try this:

Find out how to write a family member's name in hieroglyphics and then design a piece of jewelry with the new name as a gift.

Highlights:

This site loads quickly and is fun to use.

Teachers: Use this as a companion to a unit on Egypt.

See also:

Hieroglyphic Page from Seaworld

http://seaworld.org/Egypt/hiero.html

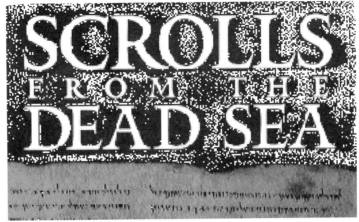

http://lcweb.loc.gov/exhibits/scrolls/

Overview:

View the ancient Dead Sea Scrolls on the Web and read about the people who hid these documents, the secrets the scrolls might reveal, and why, after their discovery in this century, the scrolls' custodians restricted access to the information contained in the scrolls. Young Bedouin shepherds searching for a goat in the Judean Desert discovered these scrolls in 1947. After entering a cave, they found jars filled with ancient scrolls. Thanks to their initial discovery, you can experience a taste of this old world at this site. Leap into the Qumran community 2,000 years ago and delve into the history of this interesting archaeological discovery. Interesting parts of the exhibit include images of artifacts from the Qumran community including the following:

- textiles
- pottery
- jugs
- basketry
- combs
- vases
- wooden objects

Try this:

Using papyrus and a pen, write your own scroll and ask a friend or family member to solve the mystery in your text. (Make sure your message opens secrets to the universe!)

Highlights:

This online, virtual museum gives you an opportunity to view a world-famous collection from the comfort of your home.

See also:

Ancient Sites.com

http://www.ancientsites.com/

The Seven Wonders of the Ancient World

Seven Wonders of the Ancient World

http://ce.eng.usf.edu/pharos/wonders

Overview:

Few people can name all the Seven Wonders of the Ancient World. Poets and historians have written about these monuments with great admiration. Today, only one of the Seven Wonders still exists: The Great Pyramid of Giza. That is why these monuments from time immemorial are the subject of much mystery and speculation. Only recently, have archaeological discoveries revealed some of the mysteries surrounding these monuments for centuries.

Seven Wonders of the world:

- Pyramids of Egypt
- Hanging Gardens of Babylon
- Statue of Zeus (at Olympia, Greece)
- Temple of Artemis (at Ephesus, Greece)
- Mausoleum of Halicarnassus
- Colossus of Rhodes
- Pharos of Alexandria (ancient lighthouse)

Try this:

If you are studying Egypt in school, use this site to learn about the building of the Pyramids.

Highlights:

Go to the clickable map and check out the locations of the Seven Wonders.

There are an abundance of links in the Forgotten Wonders section.

See also:

Modern Wonders

http://ce.eng.usf.edu/pharos/wonders/modern/index.html

Mystery of the Maya

http://www.civilization.ca/membrs/civiliz/maya/mminteng.html

Overview:

Why did the Maya, at around 900 A.D., give up their kings and return to a simple lifestyle as farmers? Despite the fact that this unsolved mystery still lingers after one thousand years, there is much to learn and explore about the Mayan civilization. Their remarkable achievements include an advanced system of mathematics and calendrics (calendars), developed writing, and expert astronomers. Take a journey deep into the jungles of Mexico, Guatemala, and the Yucatan to learn about the legacy of the classic Mayan civilization.

Try this:

Take a detour to other *Exhibits on the Plaza*, and explore a variety of excellent materials produced by the Canadian Museum of Civilization.

Highlights:

A Teacher's Guide offering questions, projects, and activities is included.

The slide show found in the *Mayan Civilization* section offers excellent photographs of architecture, sculpture, costumes, and other aspects of the Mayan world.

See also:

Rabbit in the Moon

http://www.halfmoon.org/

Find information on Mayan writing, Mayan calendar, Mayan architecture, and more.

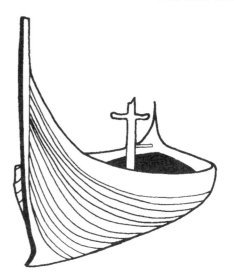

The Vikings

http://www.viking.no/e/eindex.htm

Overview:

Come to this site and find out everything about Vikings. Were Vikings really a group of seafaring men on ships seeking wealth and glory in foreign lands? Were they bloodthirsty pagans who attacked and robbed villages? No one is sure who the Vikings were or what the word "Viking" actually means. There are many theories ranging from being a people of Viken (from the Oslo fjord area in Scandinavia) to being a cove-searching people.

Take the opportunity to learn about Vikings at this site and click on the main menu to find:

- Everyday Life
- Viking Travels
- The Viking Heritage
- Viking Regions, Countries and Places
- Famous Vikings

Try this:

Follow the route of Viking movements at the *Travels* link. Test yourself on geography and see if you can identify places on the map with their modern English names.

Highlights:

This site provides a general understanding about the Vikings.

Find out the basic things that the Vikings needed in life.

See also:

The World of the Vikings

http://www.pastforward.co.uk/vikings/index.html

Creatures & Crawlers

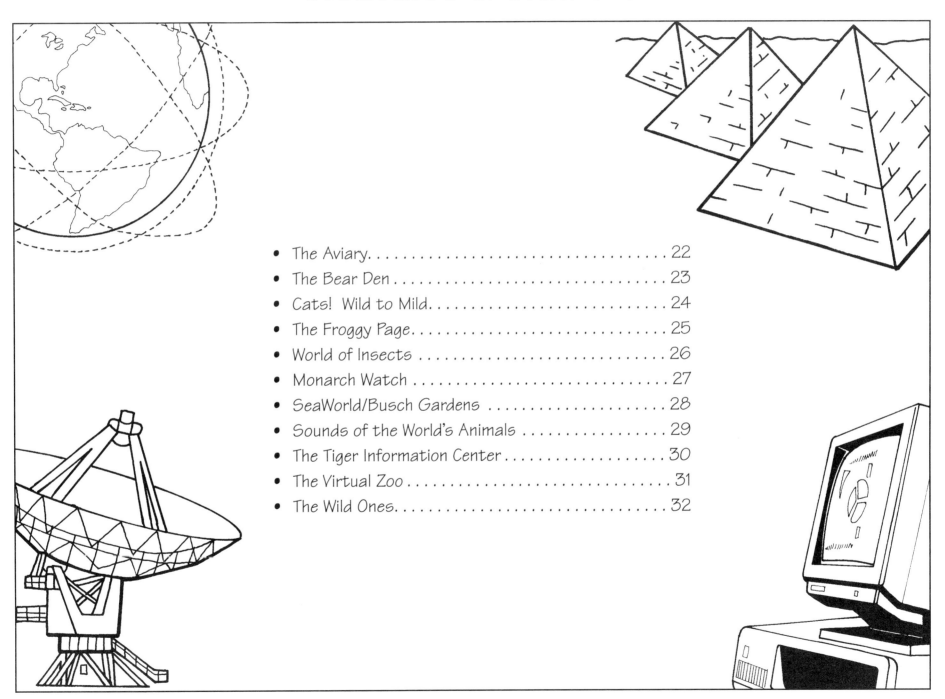

If you love birds . . . *Welcome Home!*

the *Aviary*
your avian
info center

Your complete information resource for birds!

http://theaviary.com

Overview:

Welcome to this informative and richly illustrated site dedicated to everything you would want to know about birds. If you love birds, don't pass up this comprehensive information resource about one of nature's most graceful and beautiful creations.

Click *Birding*, *The Aviary*, and find tidbits on wild and domestic birds, birding events, bird migration, bird anatomy, bird flight, bird links, resources, supplies, free clip art, bird postcards, wildflowers, pet birds, mailing lists, newsgroups, and teacher and parent resources.

- -

Try this:

Follow the link for *Types of Birds* and find information on over 100 different types of birds. Use this information as a starting point for a report.

Go to the *Post Office* and choose from over 100 free birding postcards to send to a friend or family member.

Highlights:

A massive amount of free clip art is available at this site. Use it for a *HyperStudio* slide show of our feathered friends.

See also:

Audubon Society's WatchList 4Kids

http://www.audubon.org/bird/watch/kids/index.html

Peterson Birds Online

http://www.petersononline.com/birds/month/

http://www.nature-net.com/bears/index.html

Overview:

Did you know that a bear cub is about the size of a squirrel when it is born? Or that bears stand on their hind legs to smell and see better? Find out interesting tidbits like these and more at this site featuring your furry pals, the bears! Here you will find everything you ever wanted to know about bears, including news updates, information, photographs, and other entertaining information.

A list of eight species of bears is provided.

- Brown and Grizzly Bears
- American Black Bears
- Polar Bears
- Giant Pandas

- Asiatic Black Bears
- Spectacled Bears
- Sloth Bears
- Sun Bears

Click on the name of any of these bears to find information on population, vital statistics, physical characteristics, diet, home range, reproduction, and hibernation.

- -

Try this:

Check out the *Cub Den*, a section of the Web site for younger readers that contains *Ten Facts About Bears, Amazing Facts About Bears,* and *Books for Young Readers.*

Highlights:

An excellent bibliography of bear books is provided.

This site is colorful, and informative and can be used for beginning or intermediate readers.

See also:

Koalas at Lone Pine Koala Sanctuary

http://www.koala.net/

Cats! Wild to Mild

http://www.lam.mus.ca.us/cats/

Overview:

Visit this "purrfect" site which features America's number one pet, the cat. From cat behavior, cat biology, cat history, and cat conservation to Cat Lotto (a game)and working with cats, this site is packed with enough information to satisfy any cat enthusiast!

If you are interested in finding information about a particular cat breed, click on Egypt & *Domestication*, and then *36 Flavors*. A list of domestic cat breeds with hyperlinks will provide you with the breed profile, attractive photographs, as well as related links.

- -

Try this:

Are you up to a challenge? Then go to *Cat Facts* and play Smiley the Cat's flash-card game. To play, click on the picture of the cat and try to answer the question that appears. Click a second time, and the answer will appear.

Highlights:

A complete teacher's guide is available.

Produced by the Natural History Museum of Los Angeles, this site is very informative and graphically pleasing.

See also:

The Cat Fanciers' Association

http://www.cfainc.org/

http://frog.simplenet.com/froggy/

Overview:

Do you like frogs? If you do, visit this site! Everything having to do with frogs is here, including the following:

- Froggy Pictures
- Froggy Sounds
- Froggy Tales
- Songs of the Frog
- Scientific Amphibian
- Famous Frogs
- Net Frogs

Try this:

Click on *Scientific Amphibian* and take part in a virtual frog dissection. (This is not for the tender hearted!)

Highlights:

Froggy Sounds gives you a sample of the different sounds frogs make.

Many froggy graphics can be found at this site.

See also:

The Lily Pond

http://www.thelilypad.org/

The Interactive Frog Dissection

http://curry.edschool.Virginia.EDU/go/frog/

http://www.earthlife.net/insects

Overview:

Welcome to the Wonderful World of Insects, a site loaded with information about the world's most successful life form. From ladybirds to spiders, and from grasshoppers to earwigs, you are sure to locate loads of facts about any insect beneath your feet or over your head!

Use the jump menu, "A short index of the files of this site," to choose a topic and browse through hundreds of items, including general information about each insect, a selection of graphics, a bibliography, and links to other Web sites.

Kids: If this page is too confusing, follow the link to *The Bug Club*. This part of the site is dedicated to young people who "find insects and other creepy crawlies interesting and even fascinating"!

Try this:

Check out *Bug Pets* at *The Bug Club* and find out how to take care of these miniature pets. Follow links to the *Invertebrate Care* sheets to prepare for your future with a pet insect!

Highlights:

A glossary is provided.

Information on classification of the insect orders is excellent.

See also:

O. Orkin Insect Zoo

http://www.orkin.com/html/o.orkin.html

The Microbe Zoo

http://commtechlab.msu.edu/sites/dlc-me/zoo/

http://www.MonarchWatch.org/

Overview:

How do monarch butterflies move across the continent; do they move in certain directions or take specific routes? How is their migration influenced by weather? To answer these and other questions, the Monarch Watch Outreach Program was created at the University of Kansas.

This site, designed as a companion to the program, offers great ideas, projects, and graphics about butterflies. *The Multimedia Gallery* gives monarch watchers a place where they can share their experiences online through artwork, essays, and photographs. At *Monarch Biology*, read about the monarch lifecycle from egg to larva to pupa to adult. Visit *Research Projects* and look at projects that are particularly interesting for students.

- -

Try this:

Follow the tips in *Butterfly Gardening* and create a garden which will attract monarchs.

Highlights:

Teaching materials are available at this site.

Use this site for a school research project.

See also:

Children's Butterfly Site

http://www.mesc.usgs.gov/butterfly/Butterfly.html

http://www.seaworld.org/

Overview:

Come visit SeaWorld and find lots of interesting information about animals. Need quick facts about an aquatic animal? Visit *Animal Bytes*. Need to find answers to common questions about animal life? Click on *Ask Shamu*. Looking for up-to-date information about SeaWorld? Try *Animal News*.

Another great place to visit at this site is *Just for Fun!* You can try out activities on *Egypt*, go to *Key West*, or follow scientists in *Antarctica*.

A fabulous resource at SeaWorld is its animal database that includes the following:

- Baleen Whales
- Beluga Whales
- Birds of Prey
- Bottlenose Dolphins
- Endangered Species
- Flamingoes
- Gorillas
- Harbor Seals
- Killer Whales
- Manatees

Try this:

Click on *Aquariums as a Hobby*, located in the menu on the left side of the screen, and create your own aquarium at home.

Highlights:

A wealth of animal facts can be found here.

Teacher information and guides are offered to enhance classroom activities.

See also:

Monterey Bay Aquarium

http://www.mbayaq.org/

Zoom Whales

http://www.EnchantedLearning.com/subjects/whales/

Sounds of the World's Animals

http://www.georgetown.edu/cball/animals/animals.html

Overview:

What does a bird say? It's "pip" in Danish, "tweet-tweet" in English, and "chunchun" in Japanese. How about a rooster? It's "cocorico" in French, "ake-e-ake-ake" in Thai, and "chicchirichiii" in Italian!   At this site have fun learning how people all over the world—20 languages altogether—describe the sounds animals make.

Try this:

Play a game with your friends. Choose an animal from the site and then take turns guessing what sound the animal makes in different languages.

Highlights:

This site has a simple menu. Choose sounds listed by the animal or by the language. Also included for young readers is *Spelling the Sounds of the World's Animals.*

See also:

Just Cows

http://www.arrakis.es/~eledu/justcows.htm

The Tiger Information Center

http://www.5tigers.org

Overview:

Visit the Tiger Information Center and find loads of valuable information, photographs, and fine interactive materials about tigers. Start at the *All About Tigers* section and find quick facts at *Tiger Basics*. Then follow the links to *Five Tiger Subspecies*, *Tigers in Zoos*, and *Tigers in the Media*.

Take a fast trip to the Cubs' n' Kids page and read about Tigers in Trouble or play some games.

An appealing part of this site is at Tiger Adventures where you can become involved in online simulation games that draw you into the world of tiger ecology. For example, try any of the following:

- Survive—You are a Bengal tiger and must survive in the wild.
- Tracking the Tiger Trade—Travel to India to capture tiger poachers.
- Tiger on the Loose—Help the police track an escaped tiger.
- Zoo Tiger—Design a zoo exhibit to house a runaway tiger.

Try this:

Join a conservation organization and see what you can do to help save tigers.

Use the *Tiger Basics* section as a starting point for a report on tigers.

Highlights:

Virtual experts offer tiger advice, and simulated newspapers report the results.

Teacher Resources will direct you to grade-level materials.

See also:

Learning All About Tigers

http://www.tigerlink.com/read@tigers.html

Welcome TO THE VIRTUAL ZOO

http://library.advanced.org/tq-admin/month.cgi

Overview:

Take a journey to the Virtual Zoo and visit *Monkey Island, Cat's Corner, Amazing Aviary, Ocean Life, African Animals, Pandas,* and more. This site offers you a lively excursion to the zoo. Start at the virtual map (an X marks "You are here") and click on your section of interest. The Amphibians, for example, include *frogs, toads, salamanders, newts,* and *sirens.* At African Animals visit *antelopes, cheetahs, elephants, giraffes, hippopotami, hyenas,* and *zebras.* Finally, stroll over to the *Cat's Corner* and watch frolicking *jaguars, leopards, lions,* and *cheetahs.*

Try this:

Only a Virtual Zoo could offer an area for extinct species! Check this one out for visits with the *Cynognathus, Dinosaurs, Mammoth,* and *Saber-Tooth Cat.*

Highlights:

Color photographs and sound clips are integrated into this wonderful zoo.

This site provides a good database of animals.

See also:

The Birmingham Zoo

http://www.birminghamzoo.com/

http://www.thewildones.org

Overview:

The Wild Ones offers an exciting opportunity for children, teachers, and conservation professionals in countries around the world to work together to preserve endangered species. Each section at this site is designed to improve survival prospects for endangered species. Click on *Scientists* and meet people who protect endangered animals, visit *Projects* and view students' work, or read the *Wild Times*, an online newsletter with animal updates.

You can gather information about endangered animals at *The Wild Ones Animal Index*. For each animal you will find information in the following categories: general animal description, habits, threats to survival and defending the animal against extinction. Some animals covered are the following:

- Sandhill Crane
- Scarlet Macaw
- Poison Arrow Frog
- American Alligator

- Green Iguana
- Sea Turtles
- Fruit Bats
- Jaguar

- Asian Elephant
- Red Ruffed Lemur

Try this:

Become a member of The Wild ones and share your observations, research, artwork, or creative writing in *the Wild Times*, a newsletter.

Highlights:

The Teacher Connection includes classroom, schoolyard, and field trip activities as well as pedagogical articles.

See also:

Rain Forest Action Network

http://www.ran.org/

Cards, Creativity, & Celebrations

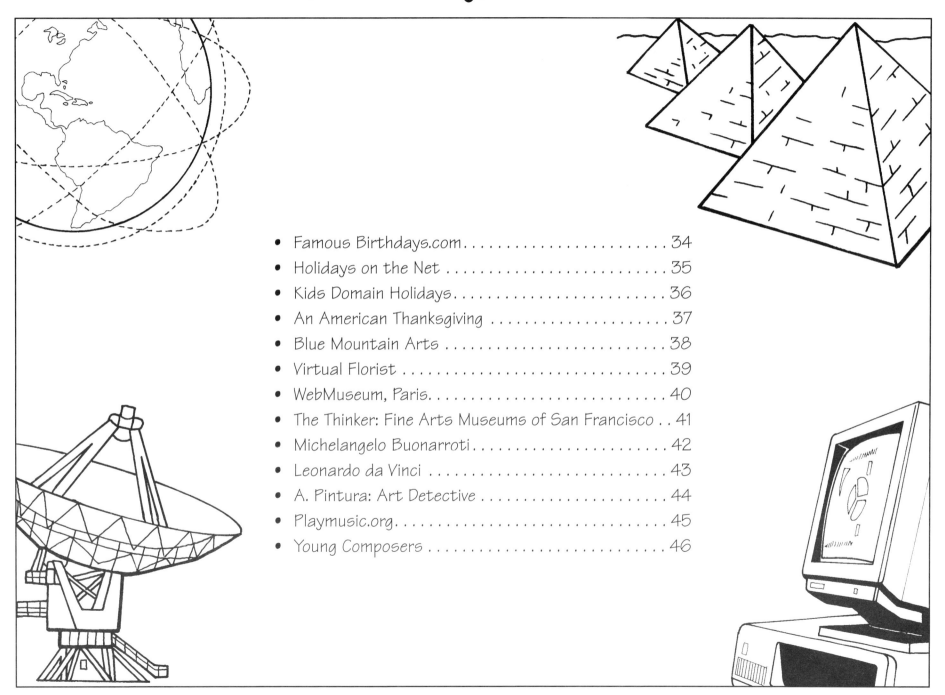

http://www.famousbirthdays.com

Overview:

Keeping up to date on birthdays is no longer a chore once you visit this site. At this quirky, yet entertaining birthday page, celebrate your birthday and famous people's birthdays by participating in several online birthday-related activities:

- Click on *Today's Birthdays* and find out who was born on this day.
- Find out who else was born on your birthday.
- Look at birthday listings of famous people by the month or year.
- Take a birthday quiz.

- Read birthday jokes.
- Check out birthdays of sports figures, writers, and Nobel and Pulitzer winners.
- Look up birthday listings by first or last names.

Before leaving this site, visit the *Other Favorite Birthday Sites*. Included are not only birthday-related sites but also movie databases, actor and actress links along with an autograph database, rock & roll sites, and more!

Try this:

Use the *Free Birthday Coupons* as gifts for friends or family members.

Sports buffs, use this site to find information on your favorite athlete.

Highlights:

Use the search box to find a famous name at this Web site.

This site uses a simple, kid-friendly interface.

See also:

dMarie Time Capsule

http://dmarie.com/timecap/

Input your birthday information and receive a screen full of information about that day in history.

http://www.holidays.net

Overview:

Holidays on the Net is a terrific site for celebrating your favorite holiday. Enjoy a combination of animation, audio, video, and colorful graphics for each holiday. Try activities or craft projects, read stories, or learn about religious traditions.

You can choose a holiday from the menu, browse through the holiday listings and descriptions, or check the days and dates of holidays. This site includes a range of holidays from Jewish Passover and High Holy Days to Christian Easter and Muslim Ramadan. Of course, Mother's Day and Father's Day are included in the collection, along with Thanksgiving, Martin Luther King Jr. Day, and Independence Day.

Try this:

Register with the *Holiday Calendar* and receive holiday e-mail reminders.

Send a friend or family member a holiday greeting card!

Highlights:

This is a colorful and kid-friendly site.

Teachers: Find out how you can use this site in your classroom.

See also:

Holidays and Celebrations by NOBLE (North of Boston Library Exchange)

http://www.noblenet.org/year.htm

http://www.kidsdomain.com/holiday/index.html

Overview:

Holidays are more enjoyable than ever with these great activities and projects at Kids Domain. There are lots of creative ideas at this site, and for every holiday there is a diverse menu. Celebrate *Valentine's Day* with some great clip art and then deliver e-cards to your family and friends. *Father's Day* includes great gift-making ideas, and Easter offers a virtual *Adopt a Lil Chick* option. Browse through this site before every holiday and get ready to celebrate!

- -

Try this:

Go to *Fall Icons* and download the pictures. Add them to your school newspaper or to a writing project.

Visit *Earth Day* and follow directions for making coffee ground fossils.

Highlights:

Each holiday is updated one to two months before the actual holiday occurs.

Excellent gift-making ideas are included along with creative gift-wrapping instructions.

Links are provided to other holiday sites.

See also:

Holidays at Billy Bear's Playground

http://www.billybear4kids.com/holidays/fun.htm

http://www.night.net/thanksgiving/

Overview:

Go to this site about Thanksgiving, the American holiday in November which reminds us to give thanks for all that we have, and find information on its history and traditions. This site recounts the first Thanksgiving at Plymouth when the Pilgrims and Native Americans shared their winter feast together. It also includes original Thanksgiving documents such as these:

- Mayflower Compact of 1620
- Peace Treaty with Massasoit, 1621
- First Thanksgiving Proclamation, 1676
- George Washington's 1789 Thanksgiving Proclamation
- Abraham Lincoln's 1863 Thanksgiving Proclamation

For a little entertainment, click on *Thanksgiving Fun* and find special certificates to download and color, stories, songs, poetry, games, and more!

Try this:

Want to help with the cooking this year? Try some of the recipes at *Thanksgiving Feast* and surprise your family with some great-tasting dishes!

Highlights:

This site provides a balance of serious historical information as well as playful interactive fun.

See also:

Caleb Johnson's Mayflower Web Pages

http://members.aol.com/calebj/mayflower.html

Blue Mountain Arts

http://www2.bluemountain.com/

Overview:

Brighten someone's day with a personalized card from this site... for free!

The process is simple. Once arriving at this site, follow these steps:

1. Browse through the ever-expanding categories of cards:
   - Holidays
   - Events & Milestones
   - Family
   - Comfort & Encouragement
   - Earth, Animals & Plants
   - Arts & Literature
   - Religions & Nations

2. Select your card.

3. Fill out the To: and From: information in the form.

4. Type a personal message in the box.

5. Preview your card.

6. Send it.

Now a special someone is having a happier day!

(Holidays are included for every celebration you can think of, including: Pet Day, Groundhog Day, Chinese New Year, Purim, and Mardi Gras.)

Try this:

Instead of mailing invitations for your birthday party via "snail-mail," gather your friends' e-mail addresses and use this site for creating and sending electronic invitations.

Highlights:

The musical accompaniment gives a special touch to each card.

Animations, colors, and designs are very creative.

See also:

Free Electronic Postcard

http://www.electronicpostcards.com/

http://www.virtualflorist.com

Overview:

There is no better way to show someone you care than to send a lovely bouquet of flowers. For Mother's Day, birthdays, or special occasions, visit this site and e-mail a friend or family member some virtual flowers for free!

To send your bouquet follow these steps:

1. Click on *Send a FREE Virtual Flower Bouquet.*

2. Choose an image from the display and click on the one you'd like to send.

3. Type a message and fill in the subject line and the e-mail address of the recipient.

4. Check what you've written by clicking on the *Preview Your Virtual Bouquet* button.

5. If you are pleased with your card, click the *Send the Free Virtual Bouquet button.*

Warning: Do not click on Send Real Flowers because those cost money!

- -

Try this:	Highlights:	See also:
Don't wait for a special occasion to send flowers. Surprise a friend by sending virtual flowers on any day of the year!	This site is simple, kid-friendly, and always brings a smile to those who receive its images!	Free Web Cards http://www.freewebcards.com/

WebMuseum, Paris

http://metalab.unc.edu/wm/

Overview:

Enter the WebMuseum, a veritable treasure chest of art and culture, and explore this fabulous collection of works of art. Begin your visit in the Special Exhibitions. Here you will find two links, one for *Cézanne* and the other for medieval art. Choose either one. Next, click on *Famous Paintings*, found in the *General Exhibition Area*, to view some of the great masterpieces of all times listed by artist or by theme. Scroll through a few of the themes, which include the following:

- the Gothic period
- Baroque
- Cubism
- Italian Renaissance
- Impressionism
- Pop Art

Visit the *Artist Index* and select Western masters from Giotto to Pollock or non-Western artists mainly from Japan. No matter which route you explore, this site is clearly presented, accurate, and a great resource for your art-hopping pleasure!

Try this:

Select *Seurat* from the *Artist Index* and then click on *The Circus*. Look at this painting carefully and see if you can tell how he painted this piece (he used small dots of contrasting colors). Create your own painting of a circus using this dot method!

Highlights:

Each artist page provides short biographies and images.

For better viewing, enlarge any work of art by clicking on its graphic image.

See also:

Museums of Paris

http://www.paris.org/Musees/

Directory of Artists at Yahoo

http://dir.yahoo.com/Arts/Artists/Masters/

http://www.thinker.org/

Overview:

The Fine Arts Museums of San Francisco presents a spectacular art imagebase as a growing, searchable catalog of their painting, drawing, etching, sculpture, porcelain, silver, glass, furniture, and textiles collections. At this site you will find 50% of the collection from the De Young and Legion of Honor museums online, which adds up to thousands and thousands of artistic images!

Try this:

Click on *Exhibitions* and then *Picasso and the War Years.* Then take the opportunity to view the *Slide Preview* of this exhibit to explore Picasso's artistic responses to the events from the Spanish Civil War through the Nazi occupation of France.

Highlights:

Teachers' resources and publications are available that further enable classroom preparation for museum visitations.

See also:

Art for Kids

http://artforkids.tqn.com/kids/artfork ids/

Fine art history, art projects, and more.

MICHELANGELO BUONARROTI
1475   1564

ENTER

http://www.michelangelo.com/buonarroti.html

Overview:

Meet Michelangelo, one of the greatest painters and sculptors of all time. This site provides an introduction to this famous Florentine artist, leading you from his early life through his final days. Here is your opportunity to visit Italy through Michelangelo's well-known works of art.

Read about:

- The David
- The Sistine Chapel
- The Laurentian Library
- The Last Judgement
- St. Peter's Basilica

This site is full of interesting historical tidbits such as Michelangelo's early life in Florence studying sculpture at the Medici Gardens and then, later, his difficult relationship with Pope Julius II as he painted the ceiling of the Sistine Chapel.

Try this:

Follow the hyperlinks from this page and take a fabulous tour of Michelangelo's work. Outstanding graphics are included at this site for your viewing enjoyment.

Highlights:

Check out the digitized five-minute video showing how IBM scientists and an eminent Renaissance art historian collaborated to reconstruct Michelangelo's Florentine Pieta.

See also:

The Uffizi Gallery in Florence

http://www.mega.it/eng/egui/monu/ufu.htm

Leonardo da Vinci

http://www.mos.org/leonardo/

Overview:

Experience the creations of this famous Italian Renaissance painter and inventor, Leonardo da Vinci. Although he is best known for his paintings, Leonardo conducted dozens of experiments and created futuristic inventions.

Take the opportunity to visit four different sections at this site:

1. Inventor's Workshop
2. Leonardo's Perspective
3. Leonardo: Right to Left
4. What, Where, When?

Try this:

Visit the *Leonardo Right to Left* page, and then try to write your signature in cursive from right to left. This is quite challenging!

Highlights:

After exploring *The Inventor's Toolbox*, try going to *Gadget Anatomy* and see if you can correctly choose which machine parts match the gadgets displayed.

Many aspects of da Vinci's genius are presented at this site.

See Also:

da Vinci's Inventions

http://www.lib.stevens-tech.edu/collections/davinci/inventions/index.html

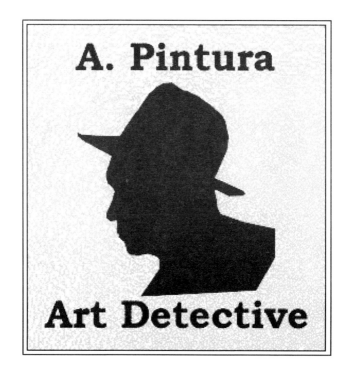

http://www.eduweb.com/pintura/

Overview:

Grandpa died and left an old dusty painting to Miss Fiona Featherduster. Miss Featherduster wants to know if it is valuable, so she seeks the advice of Art Detective A. Pintura. To answer her question, join this mysterious twosome and discover who painted Grandpa's painting. Could it be Raphael, Titian, Millet, Van Gogh, Gauguin, or Picasso? Take the opportunity at this site to use your keen sense of awareness while viewing exquisite paintings from some of the world's most famous artists.

Try this:

Check out the newest project, *ArtEdventures with Carmine Chameleon*, by clicking on this link.

Highlights:

Designed by Educational Web Adventures, this interactive site offers an online journey through the art world.

See also:

Inside Art

http://www.eduweb.com/insideart/index.html

Explore a painting from the inside out.

Reprinted by permission of Playmusic.org. ©1999 American Symphony Orchestra League

http://www.playmusic.org/

Overview:

If you are looking for entertaining and imaginative ways to develop your interest in classical music, visit *Playmusic.org*, the site where you can explore the many dimensions of an orchestra and even gain a sense of what it's like to be part of one. Begin at the *Main Stage* to discover each different section of the orchestra. Click on *brass, percussion, woodwinds,* or *strings* and listen to orchestral passages featuring, for example, how the flute sounds playing part of the Nutcracker Suite by Tchaikovsky. Then visit the *Backstage* where you'll find sections about composers and musicians, as well as links to other music sites. There are lots of opportunities to listen to music at this site, and kids can gain a good understanding of how orchestras work.

- -

Try this:

Try some of the clever games included for each orchestral section. For example, help Dr. Strad put his violin back together at *Strings,* or match the sound with the correct instrument at *Name That Woodwind.*

Highlights:

This is a fully interactive site offering a wide variety of listening experiences.

See also:

Children's Music Web

http://www.childrensmusic.org

Check out *Pipsqueaks* for sing-along songs or *Musicians List* for information on musicians.

http://www.youngcomposers.com/

Overview:

This is a great site for aspiring musicians. Kids send musical compositions to this site, and when you click on *New Releases* or *Earlier Works*, you will find a list of their pieces available for your listening pleasure! Also available is a selection of pieces by famous composers.

Music is listed by category:

- Baroque/Classical
- Choral/Religious
- Jazz
- Modern

- New Age
- Rock/Blues
- Romantic/Impressionist
- World Music

Note: You need Javascript and frames for this site.

Try this:

Click on *Play Music Match* and see if you can name that tune! Listen to music by famous composers and see if you can identify the composer who wrote each piece.

Highlights:

This site offers numerous musical works from which to choose.

See Also:

ClassicalNet: A Guide to Composer Data & Works Lists

http://www.classical.net/music/composer/

Mysteries, Tales, & Magazines

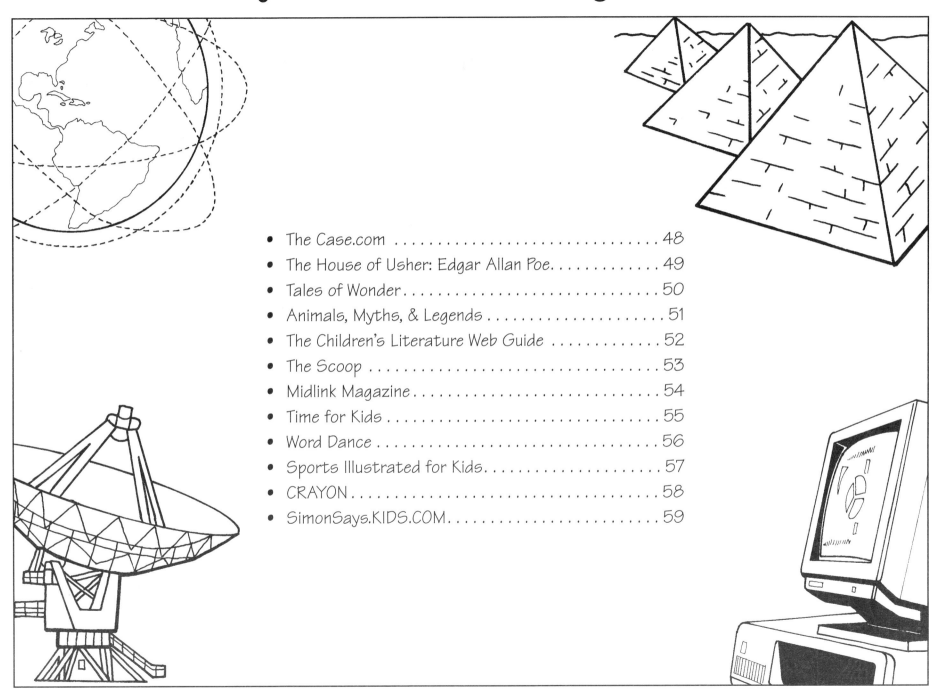

http://www.TheCase.com/kids

Overview:

Everyone loves a good mystery! For entertainment and engaging stories, go to The Case.com. At this site you can create your own mysteries, read scary stories, and try out magic tricks.

Special sections feature the following:

- Solve-it—Try a solve-it-yourself mini-mystery.
- Chiller—A chilling tale will scare you.
- Quick-solve—Can you figure it out?
- Magic Trick—Amaze your friends.

- Nancy Drew.com—Visit everyone's favorite teen sleuth.
- Writing Contest—Write a mystery about the mysterious photo of the week.
- Vote-n-Solve—Play an interactive mystery game.

At this site, you have the opportunity to submit solutions to mini-mysteries and to create original stories.

Try this:

Write a mini-mystery and enter the *Mysterious Writing Contest* (make sure you read the guidelines).

Highlights:

Lesson plans and ideas are included for using mysteries in the classroom.

For mystery buffs this is not be missed!

See also:

History of the Mystery Quiz

http://www.MysteryNet.com/learn/sites

Take this quiz and find out exactly how much you know about mysteries!

http://www.comnet.ca/~forrest/

Overview:

This eerie site featuring Edgar Allan Poe greets you with the "Adams Family Waltz" by Marc Shaiman from the 1991 movie. Once entering Poe's world, take a journey into the works and life of this macabre author and poet. Visit his homes and burial site under *Favorite Haunts*, read Poe's poems, or find information on his life and interests.

- -

Try this:

"The Raven," Poe's most famous poem, is often recognized by the lines in its first stanza. Click on this poem and make an attempt at memorizing this verse. Recite it for your friends before Halloween for a little fun!

Highlights:

This is a creepy and creative portrayal of Edgar Allan Poe.

See also:

The Edgar Allan Poe Society of Baltimore

http://www.eapoe.org/

http://members.xoom.com/darsie/tales/index.html

Overview:

Richard Darsie has compiled fairy tales, folk tales, and mythology from around the world at this site. If you are studying one country, you can print these stories to use in your classroom. Stories are available from the following countries:

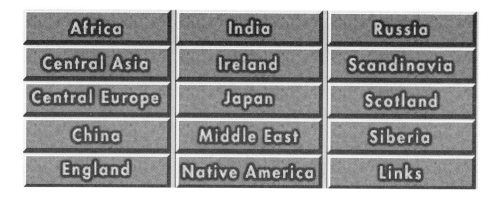

Africa	India	Russia
Central Asia	Ireland	Scandinavia
Central Europe	Japan	Scotland
China	Middle East	Siberia
England	Native America	Links

Try this:

Read "The Comrades" from the *Native American* section. Put on a play of this story and pretend that you are a set designer. Make sketches of trees, bushes, water, buildings, wildlife and the time of day or night for the different sets.

Highlights:

This is a great multi-cultural collection of stories. Tricksters from India and Africa provide humor and entertainment.

See also:

Aesop's Fables

http://www.cruzio.com/~seaweb/corbin/aesop.html

Author Online! Aaron Shepard's Home Page

http://www.aaronshep.com

Animals, Myths, & Legends

http://www.planetozkids.com

Overview:

Come visit Oban the Knowledge Keeper and his fellow storytellers who take you through the world of myths and legends. Discover Oban's collection of games, activities, and folklore and explore different cultures from around the world. This site presents common themes found in stories from various cultures of the world and invites you to learn about the myths and legends of your country and other cultures.

Try this:

Select *Channel 1*, and click on *Animals Myths, and Legends*. At this screen, go to the *Playroom* and try *Oban's Brain Torture* crossword puzzle. Then, do a word search or travel to another playroom in the Internet universe!

Highlights:

Find a legend or myth about an animal from your country, write it in your own words in an e-mail, and send it to Oban. He'll put some of the legends he receives on his page!

See also:

Myths and Fables

http://www.afroam.org/children/myths/myths.html

The Children's Literature Web Guide

http://www.acs.ucalgary.ca/~dkbrown

Overview:

The Children's Literature Web Guide (CLWG), developed by David Brown of the University of Calgary, gathers together and categorizes resources related to books for children and young adults. This excellent and highly-rated site organizes the best of the Web, compiles book award lists from print sources (Newbery/Caldecott Awards), publishes submissions from kids, offers book reviews, stories, author information, teaching ideas, and a host of other features.

Try this:

Go to *What We're Reading* and find out what the author of this Web site likes to read.

Check out the current Newbery winners. Do you agree with the winning selections?

Highlights:

This is a great site for teachers, librarians, parents, avid readers, and kids!

The list of *Best Books* provides an invaluable resource.

See also:

Candlelight Stories

http://www.CandlelightStories.com/

Children s Book News

http://www.friend.ly.net/scoop

Overview:

Welcome to The Scoop, an electronic publication, where you'll find reviews of children's books, plenty of activities, information about books, interviews with authors, and more.

Browse through award-winning books, biographies, and favorite links and then check out the *Activity Center* including:

- Arts & Crafts—Build a birdbath.
- Contests—Try the World Almanac for Kids Contest.
- Cooking for Kids—Bake yummy taste treats.
- Jokes & Riddles—Share rib-ticklers and knee-slappers.
- Science Projects—Be a science professor.
- Sewing Project—Design great crafts.
- The Scoop Coloring Book—Enter the coloring contest.

Try this:

Use the book reviews as a guide next time you want to choose a book to read from the library.

Highlights:

The Scoop Resource Page offers high-quality literature links on the Web.

Read the current issue of The Scoop or search for older issues in the archives.

See also:

Berit's Best Sites for Children

http://www.beritsbest.com/

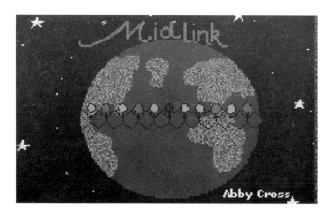

Midlink Magazine©

The Digital Magazine for Kids By Kids

http://longwood.cs.ucf.edu/~MidLink/

Overview:

Midlink Magazine, established in 1994, is an award winning electronic magazine for kids and by kids in the middle grades. It includes exemplary Web sites for teachers and students, as well as exciting and interactive projects with student-created content. The site encourages students to publish their own work and is a fine example of an effective classroom design on the Net.

Explore this site by reading new articles, and then meander over to the archives and browse through older editions of Midlink. Don't forget to check out *Cool Schools* to find some of the most interesting wired schools.

Try this:

Tell your older brother or sister about *Secondary Roads*, the section of Midlink Magazine for students in the upper grades.

Go to *Best Web Sites Honor Roll* and surf through A+ sites. The section entitled *Just for Fun* is quite enticing!

Highlights:

Resources for teachers include information on Acceptable Use Policies, Best Web Sites, *Search Tools, Copyright Guidelines*, and much more!

See also:

The Vocal Point

http://bvsd.k12.co.us/schools/cent/Newspaper/Newspaper.html

http://www.timeforkids.com/TFK/index.html

Overview:

Enjoy the kids' version of *Time Magazine* in its online form. This site focuses on kids in the news as well as other news stories that would be of interest to kids. This colorful and graphic news source will hold your interest while providing comprehensive articles in the following categories:

- Who's News
- Cartoon
- Kids Talk Back
- Multimedia
- In the News
- Top 5
- Search TFK/Archive

Check out *Multimedia* and read about fascinating topics like the *Robotlab* (you can try building your own robot), the exploration of Mars, or *Diamond History Fast Facts!*

Try this:

Send e-mail to Time for Kids and express your opinion about a news issue covered in this magazine.

Highlights:

The searchable archive provides access to previous articles according to subject or date.

The magazine is available according to grade level: Click on Grades 2-3 or Grades 4-6.

See also:

Kids Magazine

http://www.thetemple.com/KidzMagazine/

Letters   Field Trip   World Word   Haiku Corner   Grab Bag

http://www.worddance.com/

Overview:

Visit the home of *Word Dance* magazine online, and become inspired with the variety of creative opportunities provided at this site. Kids in kindergarten through eighth grade can read samples of student-created stories, articles, and poetry, and view artwork as well. The site is divided into sections which include the following:

- Letters
- Field Trip
- World Word
- Haiku Corner
- Grab Bag
- Art Gallery
- Kids Links
- Word Games

For some additional fun, try *Word Scramble, MadLib, Checkers, Tic-Tac-Toe,* or *Paint,* all of which can be found in the Word Games section!

Try this:

Try your hand at publishing by filling out a submission form with your own piece of writing, poetry, or art and send it to this magazine.

Highlights:

This site provides a "real world" application for language arts topics.

It is an excellent interactive site for classroom teachers.

See also:

For Young Writers

http://www.inkspot.com/young/

©Sports Illustrated for Kids

http://www.sikids.com/index.html

Overview:

Visit this colorful site with articles on famous sport greats from the NBA, NCAA, and NHL. Get quick sport updates at *Shorter Reporter* and then check out league standings, games, and the *Trivia Challenge*.

An exciting part of this site is called *Fantasy Sport* where you can play strange types of sports like these:

- Speed-O-Fantasy Racing—Rev up a NASCAR team.
- March-O-Fantasy Basketball—March into madness.
- Hoop-O-Matic Basketball—Guaranteed not to lock you out!
- Puck-O-Matic Fantasy Hockey—You shoot, you score!

As you would expect, this site offers great sports games online like *Indy Frenzy, Michael Jordan Trivia Jam, Deion v. Deion,* and more!

Try this:

Go to the magazine page and follow the clues at *Mystery Athlete* to figure out who he/she is!

Read the question sent in by a *Sports Illustrated* kid. Read it, think it over, and if you have advice to share, click on the link provided and send it in.

Highlights:

Check out the day's scores, stats, and standings at the *Stat Center*.

Good articles are included from the printed magazine version.

See also:

The Locker Room Sports for Kids!

http://members.aol.com/msdaizy/sports/locker.html

Create Your Own Newspaper
Your Personalized Internet News Service

`http://crayon.net/`

http://crayon.net

Overview:

If you are interested in news and current events, you'll want to try CRAYON, an acronym for CReate Your Own Newspaper. CRAYON automates the process of constructing a personalized, Web-based newspaper for free! To use this site, simply click on *Create Your Free Newspaper*, enter your e-mail address, and choose a password. Choose a title, motto, and layout for the paper. From there you fill out a form checking news categories you are interested in. Some of the sections follow:

- U.S. News
- Regional and Local News
- World News
- Politics

- Editorial and Opinions
- Weather Conditions and Forecasts
- Business Report
- Information and Technology Report

- Health and Fitness Roundup
- Funny Page
- Tabloid Page
- Cool Web Sites

When you are finished, select the *Create this newspaper now* button! Your newspaper will be given its own URL. Bookmark this page and go read your custom-designed paper every day!

- -

Try this:

Try modifying your paper by changing the news categories or layout. Observe your reaction to these changes and reflect on why you prefer certain types of news.

Design a separate paper for a friend.

Highlights:

Depending on your selections, the newspaper will include a current weather map for your city along with comics you enjoy.

Nearly a thousand news sources are provided.

See also:

KidNews

http://www.kidnews.com/

http://www.simonsays.com/kids

Overview:

Visit SimonSays KIDS.COM, a site designed with kids' reading interests in mind. Here you'll find information about many well-known books and authors, and you can also browse through new books that pique your interest. A favorite section of this site is at *Find a Book*. Simply type as much information as you know about a book in the search box (a title, author, subject, or series), click on *Find It!*, and a review of the book will appear on a new screen.

Try this:

Go to *Cool Stuff,* and try some of the games at this section.

Use this site to find reviews of books you'd like to read.

Highlights:

Check *New Releases* from time to time to learn about recently published books.

Teachers: Check out the *Teachers Lounge* for classroom guides.

See also:

Education Place

http://www.eduplace.com

Go to the Kids Clubhouse for some reading fun!

Find That Fact!

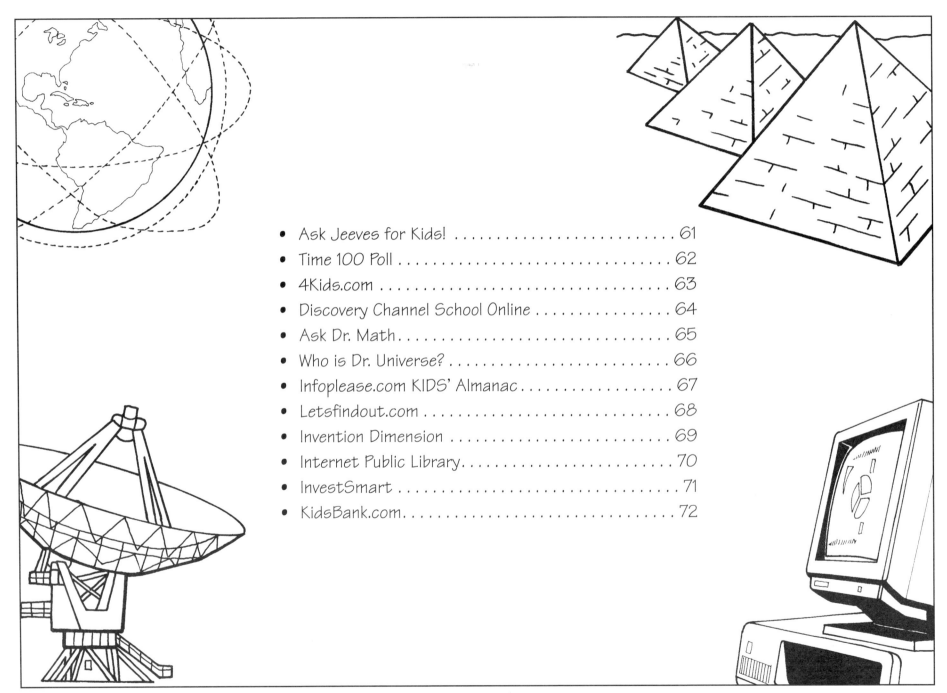

http://www.ajkids.com

Overview:

Welcome to *Ask Jeeves for Kids*, a highly-used tool among Web surfers! Why is Ask Jeeves so popular? Jeeves uses a unique search tool that lets kids ask questions on almost any subject while providing fast, easy, and safe ways to find answers.

To use *Ask Jeeves*:

1. Enter a question in plain English into the search box.
2. Jeeves will search his database and return lists of any related questions.
3. Select the question(s) that best matches your original inquiry.
4. Click on the Ask button and the answer to the question will lead to a Web page that has been reviewed by Jeeves' staff of researchers.

With thousands of question templates and millions of kid-safe researched links, it is difficult to imagine your questions won't be answered. But just in case Jeeves comes up empty handed, e-mail your question to him, and researchers will try to find an answer!

Try this:

Improve your vocabulary by clicking the *Today's Word* link on a regular basis!

Visit *Student Resources* and browse through questions that other kids have previously asked!

Highlights:

Teachers: You can ask Jeeves questions like, "Where can I find information on aquariums?" or, "Where can I find a quiz on tigers?"

See also:

Alta Vista

http://www.altavista.com

This is a search engine that allows adults to find information using a whole sentence.

Time 100 Poll

http://www.pathfinder.com/time/time100

Overview:

This site takes a look at people who have had the greatest impact on the twentieth century as selected by *Time Magazine*. This is a superb research site and is arranged in five categories:

- Leaders and Revolutionaries
- Artists and Entertainers
- Builders and Titans
- Scientists and Thinkers
- Heroes and Inspirations

Browse through these sections and find excellent biographical material.

Try this:

Submit your choice for the most influential person/people of the century and vote in the *Time 100 Poll* or *Person of the Century Poll.*

Check out the *TIME Warp* link and find out how the world has changed during this century.

Highlights:

Each category features profiles of 20 people, including audio and video clips, archival material, quizzes, time lines, and related Web sites.

See also:

Biography.com

http://www.biography.com

4Kids.Com

http://www.4kids.com/4kidshome.html

Overview:

Climb up in the 4Kids treehouse and spend your day playing, studying, researching, or reading. Click on the *toy box, bookshelf, globe, bulletin board,* or *fish bowl* and be transported to reading material, science facts, dictionaries, and games. Or go to the bottom of the page and follow the subject links:

- Entertainment
- Playroom
- Projects
- Science
- Social Studies
- Study Resources

All in all, you will find a little bit of everything at this site, all arranged to provide hours of enjoyment!

- -

Try this:

Having a boring day? Click on *Entertainment* and find a wealth of cartoon sites.

Highlights:

View some kids' home pages or class projects that have been listed on the *4Kids Projects* page.

This site provides a variety of resources designed with the elementary student in mind.

See also:

Merriam-Webster Online

http://www.m-w.com

http://school.discovery.com/

Overview:

Explore natural phenomena, go back in time, or delve into a variety of exciting themes at the *Discovery Channel School Online.* The following is just a small sample of the many enticing themes that this site offers.

For example:

- Day in History—This presents historical tidbits for every day of the year.
- Theme Week—Click on a featured theme such as World Empires, Planet of Life, Systems & Structures, and a wealth of others.
- Features—Check out a science story, sneak previews, games, and more.
- Earth Alert—Natural phenomena and disasters are featured here.
- Discussions—Find out what leading experts and peers think about a particular subject.

Try this:

Click on Features and read the most current feature story in the news.

No time to visit the zoo? Click on *Animal Cam* to see live, real-time animals in action!

Highlights:

Can't find what you need? Search Discoveryschool.com's resources by grade level, subject, and resource type.

Lessons plans for teachers include vocabulary, study questions, related Web sites, hands-on activities, and more.

See also:

The Why Files

http://whyfiles.news.wisc.edu/

Ask Dr. Math

http://forum.swarthmore.edu/dr.math/

Overview:

Here is one of the best, most complete, and highly rated math sites on the Internet. Dr. Math is a rewarding place to go when you have questions about a math problem. Simply submit questions to Dr. Math by filling out his Web form or by sending e-mail for help, and you will receive an answer to your questions via e-mail.

Dr. Math also provides an archive searchable by grade level and subject matter for elementary throughout college levels.

Try this:

Looking for an intriguing math problem? Dr. Math offers a problem of the week for the courageous student.

Highlights:

FAQ (Frequently Asked Questions) offers a comprehensive list of topics.

Excellent link to other Math Sites are provided.

See also:

Math Forum

http://forum.swarthmore.edu/

It is a great math source for students and teachers.

Featured Questions
Big answers to big questions new every other Monday.

Today's Question
A new question every day!

Previous Questions
BOTH SHORT AND LONG
A treasure chest of questions & answers!

http://www.wsu.edu/DrUniverse/

If you have lots of questions, this is the site for you. You can ask Dr. Universe almost anything. She'll answer your question herself or go to Washington State University's research team for advice. She goes to libraries, field sites, or virtually anywhere to find answers to kids' questions.

Here are some questions kids have asked:

- Why do cats hate water?
- What is a black hole?
- Why do we dream?

- Were dinosaurs just too picky?
- Why am I so tired after lunch?
- What's the point of leap year?

Your questions never end, and neither do the answers at *Ask Dr. Universe.*

- -

Try this:

Submit a question to Dr. Universe. Do your own research at the library and then compare your answer with Dr. Universe's response.

Highlights:

This is an award-winning site that is perfect for kids who want to know everything.

See also:

B. J. Pinchbeck's Homework Helper

http://www.bjpinchbeck.com/

http://kids.infoplease.com/

Overview:

This reference site designed for kids is a great resource for any report or project. Do you want to know about the tallest mountain in the world? Do you need to know which country has the fewest number of household appliances? You will find the answers to these and all kinds of questions in the online *Infoplease* almanac, encyclopedia, and dictionary.

This site is loaded with numerous topics such as:

- People
- Sports
- Fun Facts
- World
- U.S.

- Science
- Homework Center
- Word of the Day
- Today in History—for famous events
- Today's Birthday—for people's birthdays every day of the year

Try this:

Give yourself a quiz on paper money. Whose picture is on a $100 bill? $500? $1,000? Check your answers in the homework center. Did you get them right?

Highlights:

You can search this site by keyword or by subject category.

This site has a clear, well-designed interface.

See also:

A Web of Online Dictionaries

http://www.facstaff.bucknell.edu/rbeard/diction.html

http://www.letsfindout.com/

Overview:

Another great site from Knowledge Adventure, *Letsfindout.com*, is an online encyclopedia which gives you the capability to access information on a variety of subjects online. Find facts at your fingertips by using the subject search that categorizes materials according to the subject, or use the search box and enter the item(s) you wish to find!

Try this:

Click on the *Browse All* link and choose a subject you know nothing about. Take the opportunity to learn more about a new hobby, sport, or famous person.

Highlights:

The handy keyword search option has the following capabilities:

- Searching is case insensitive (you can use lowercase letters).
- AND can be used to combine words.
- A single space can be used to separate multiple keywords.

See also:

Encyclopedia.com

http://www.encyclopedia.com/home.html

"Courtesy of the Invention Dimension, Lemelson-MIT Program"

http://web.mit.edu/invent/

Overview:

Did you ever wonder who invented plastic? crayons? frozen foods? This site, created at the Massachusetts Institute of Technology (MIT), provides answers to these and other questions. The best part of this site for kids is the *Inventor of the Week* Archives. Search for inventors or inventions listed in alphabetical order.

Try this:

Do a report on an invention for your science class. Use this site for your research.

Highlights:

A thorough and well-researched database can be found here.

See also:

Inventors and Inventions at Discovery Online

http://school.discovery.com/lessonplans/programs/inventorsandinventions1/

National Inventors Hall of Fame

http://www.invent.org/book/index.html

Internet Public Library

http://www.ipl.org

Overview:

The Internet Public Library, a project of the School of Information at the University of Michigan, is the first public library of the Internet. The librarians who manage the site are committed to providing valuable and worthwhile sites to the public while also creating a useful place on the Internet.

The reference center lists resources under the following headings:

- Arts & Humanities
- Business & Economics
- Entertainment & Leisure
- Health & Medical Sciences

- Law, Government, & Political Science
- Sciences & Technology
- Social Sciences
- Associations

Check this out!

Click on the special section for youth and go to the *Reading Zone, Dewey, Science Net, Sports, Reference, Our World, USA, Art, Fun Stuff, Math Whiz* or *Health.* J. J. the Librarian at the Youth Division will help you explore these sections!

- -

Try this:

Is it time to design a project for the annual science fair at your school? Visit *Dr. Internet* and explore the *Science Fair Project Resource Guide.*

Highlights:

A special teen division caters to the research needs of high school students.

This site is an excellent source for school projects.

See also:

Pitsco's Ask an Expert

http://www.askanexpert.com

InvestSmart

http://library.thinkquest.org/10326/

Overview:

Enter InvestSmart and learn about trading stocks. This site provides an interactive stock market simulation; each player is given $100,000 virtual dollars to invest in over 5,000 companies. Buy stock on the New York Stock Exchange (NYSE), NASDAQ, or the American Stock Exchange (AMEX). You can research companies and decide which stocks to buy or sell.

Also included at this site are the following topics:

- Investment Basics—Become a millionaire by investing only $100 a month.
- Investment Lessons—Find explanations of stocks, bonds, mutual funds, and taxes.
- Real-life Examples—View portfolios of teenagers.

Try this:

Use different logon names to sign up for this game more than once and trade different stocks in each account to test out a variety of investment strategies.

Highlights:

Throw that newspaper away and keep track of your profits with the real stock and mutual fund quotes delayed by only 20 minutes.

See also:

Kids' Money

http://www.kidsmoney.org/

The New York Stock Exchange (NYSE)

http://www.nyse.com/

http://www.kidsbank.com/

Overview:

Do you spend your allowance on candy and video games? Try using money in a different way and let some new friends at Bank.com—Dollar Bill, Interest Ray, Mr. Money, and others—help you learn about saving and then discover why a bank is the best place to do it.

Look for the professor who lurks around this site, and with a click he will offer more information about a particular subject area. Ask Mr. Money offers a bulletin board where you can read questions submitted by other kids. If your question has not been answered, send it to the professor and come back the next day for an answer. Checks, the dog, will show you how to write checks, and Mr. Electronic Funds Transfer (ETF) allows you to discover how money can be moved around the world!

- -

Try this:

Click on *Calculators* and find out how much money you will need to save to become a millionaire.

Highlights:

This is a great site for the beginning saver.

See also:

Universal Currency Converter

http://www.xe.net/ucc/

Going on a trip to France? Find out what dollars are worth in francs!

Games & Whimsical Fancies

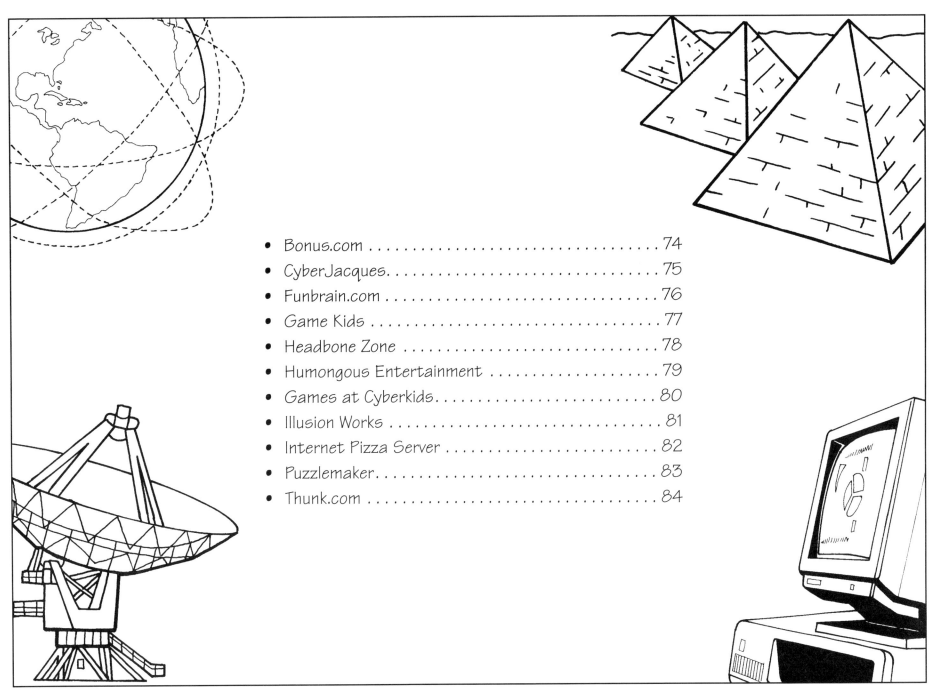

©Bonus Network Co

http://www.bonus.com

Overview:

Bonus.com is a colorful "SuperSite" offering hundreds of quality activities for kids. At first peek, it will seem as if this site offers only games, but with a second look, you will notice a site loaded with other kid-friendly experiences!   Enjoy the following sections at this site including:

- Play—Brain Games, Weekly Arcade, Sports Action, and more
- Color—Lots of great coloring pages, including Cool Art, Animal Show-Offs, and Favorite Pets
- Imagine—Adventures, Storytelling, So Strange, Fashion, and other imaginative activities
- Explore—Use this section as a homework helper and find information on dinosaurs, Earth, natural disasters, the body, heroes, and more!

Note: Bonus.com is presented in a protected environment called NetScooter® and is available in another window on your computer screen.

Try this:

Register with Bonus.com (with parental permission, of course!) to compete in contests and earn medals.

Go to *Illusions* and then *Spirals*. Make the spirals rotate by pressing the "+" key on the computer. Then look at the rotating spiral and notice how it affects your vision!

Highlights:

Educators and parents: Curriculum content is available to supplement standard lessons in a non-standard, Bonus.com entertaining style!

A range of difficulty allows kids of many ages to participate at this site.

See also:

The Electric Origami Shop

http://www.ibm.com/stretch/EOS/

CyberJacques

http://www.best.com/~joshuas/

Overview:

Meet CyberJacques, the captain of the "grizzliest, silliest site on the high seas of the Internet"! Join CyberJacques and check out his collection of games, many of which are based around pirate themes. Then lower your anchor for awhile and select a game from the list below:

Try these:

- Tangram Game
- Tile Puzzle
- Memory Matching Game

- Connect the Dots
- Plank Jumper
- What's Inside?

- Secret World II
- Hangman
- Simon Says

Note: All games require Shockwave.

Try this:

Get a stopwatch. Select a game and challenge a friend to play it in a predetermined amount of time.

Play the *Memory Matching Game.* (Make sure your images are autoloading before you start.)

Highlights:

Games are kid-friendly and provide hours of fun.

See also:

Hangman
http://www.allmIxedup.com/cgl-bin/hangman/hangman

Every wrong letter brings the stick man closer to the gallows. Nice little site.

http://www.funbrain.com

Overview:

Welcome to *FunBrain*, a collection of games for kids of all ages. This site organizes games in three ways. The first is according to age level: 6 and under, 7-10, 11-14, and 15 and up. The second is according to subject, and finally, you can browse through a pulldown menu that allows you to check out all the possibilities, including the games listed below:

- Math Baseball
- Power Football
- Shape Surveyor
- Line Jumper
- Change Maker

- Spellaroo
- Grammar Gorillas
- Piano Player
- Who Is That?
- Sign the Alphabet

Try this:

Try *Brainbowl*, a weekly current-event quiz that you can receive through e-mail or play over the Web.

Highlights:

Games include clear instructions.

Kids can choose the level of difficulty they wish to play.

See also:

Flashcards for Kids

http://www.edu4kids.com/math/

Game Kids

http://www.gamekids.com/

Overview:

Game Kids is a gathering place for kids of all ages to learn and exchange noncomputer games and activities. Each month, games, rhymes, activities, and recipes will be selected from around the world for you to download, print out, and enjoy. You are invited to submit your favorite games, stories, poetry, artwork, photographs, and recipes.

Try this:

Tired of kickball and soccer? Use this site to find other great physical education games that are kid-tested and approved.

Browse through Nail Party Games for some new inspiration!

Highlights:

Write a description of your favorite game and submit it to Game Kids.

Lots of creative ideas can be found here.

See also:

Game Kids Teens

http://www.gamekids.com/teenp1.html

http://www.headbone.com

Overview:

Enter the *Headbone Zone*, a spot where you can play captivating computer games on the Web. At this site you'll find lots of challenging scavenger hunts, puzzles, brainteasers, a game chat room, a chance to win prizes, and more!

This site features:

- hbz Voter—Check out Headbone democracy in action.
- Smirk City—Enter a town filled with laughter.
- Pojo's Digital Destiny Machine—Try this wacky gizmo.
- Hey Velma, How Come?—Check out weekly questions and answers with Velma the pig.

At Games and Prizes try:

- Rags to Riches
- FleetKids
- Hack.Back
- Mars or Bust
- Elroy PI
- Headbone Derby

There's only one rule at this site: "Be smart and use your headbone!"

Note: Most games require *Shockwave*.

- -

Try this:

If you don't have much online time, go to *Quick Games* for some fast fun.

Play *Rags to Riches* and take your shot at fortune and fame!

Highlights:

Headbone offers positive and kid-safe activities.

See also:

Imagiware's Game Zone

http://imagiware.com/games.html

http://www.humongous.com/

Overview:

At *Humongous Entertainment* play games, read comics, download Computer Goodies, and print Coloring Pages with loveable characters. Meet Pajama Sam, Freddi Fish, Junior Sports, SPY Fox, Putt-Putt, and Fatty Bear and join their irresistible world!

Each character has his own section of this fun-filled site. Simply click on one of their pictures from the menu and then roam through activities featuring that character.

Try this:

At Pajama Sam's page, click on *Wacky Weather Game* so you can check out Pajama Sam's Wacky World Wide Weather Report. To play, pick a newspaper title and headline. Then type words in the boxes and be prepared for lots of giggles!

Highlights:

This fun-packed, colorful site has a kid-friendly interface.

Lots of games, downloadable demos, and entertainment can be found here.

See also:

The Family Games Web Center

http://www.familygames.com/

Games at CyberKids

http://www.cyberkids.com/fg/index.html

Overview:

This is a favorite site for kids who love games, puzzles, and mazes!

Play a variety of interactive games such as the selections below:

- Alien Assembly
- Concentration using Egyptian Hieroglyphics
- Hippie Hockey
- Lockdown

- Music Match
- Pinball
- Why Do Birds Marry?

Note: Most games require Shockwave.

Try This:

Play *Alien Assembly* and create your own alien by choosing alien body parts with the *New* button.

Highlights:

Games and puzzles are very creative and have interesting graphics.

Have hours of fun at this site!

See also:

Learn2 Play Checkers

http://209.24.233.206/05/0501/0501.html

Illusion Works

http://www.illusionworks.com

Overview:

Visit this innovative site about illusions to understand why our brains fool us into seeing things that aren't the way they actually exist. Illusion Works offers a comprehensive collection of mind-boggling optical and sensory illusions along with detailed explanations about why they are interpreted differently by different people.

Spend many hours at Illusion Works checking out interactive demonstrations, illusion artwork, interactive puzzles, 3-D graphics, perception links, and more. Tour some of the amazing parts of this site listed below:

- Ambiguous Images
- Motion Ambiguity
- Camouflage Illusions
- Stereograms
- Tesseract
- Adelson Brightness Illusions
- Shadow Illusions
- Cross-Modal Interaction

Don't be alarmed if you see double after leaving this site. Your vision will eventually return to normal.

- -

Try this:

Click on *Interactive Demonstration* to enter the Hall of Illusions. Next select *Impossible Figures and Objects*. Take a tour of these spatially inconsistent and paradoxical shapes and gain insights as to how the brain interprets 3-D verses 2-D images. Be patient as this incredible site loads on your computer.

Highlights:

This site features examples of some of the world's leading illusion artists, including M. C. Escher, Shigeo Fukuda, Scott Kim, Sandro Del Prete, and others.

Note: At the writing of this book, the introductory level was still under construction.

See also:

Grand Illusions

http://www.grand-illusions.com/

Exploratorium Online Exhibits

http://www.exploratorium.edu/exhibits/

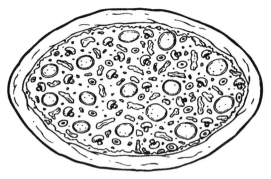

Internet Pizza Server

http://www.ecst.csuchico.edu/~pizza/pizzaweb.html

Overview:

Stop at this site and order a piping hot virtual pizza! Select the size and then choose from a menu of toppings, including the following:

- Meats
- Veggies
- Breakfast
- Sporting Goods

- Junk Food
- Hardware
- Misc

You can almost smell the yummy hammers and pop tarts. Let your imagination go wild at this site and try not to let your virtual appetite get out of hand.

Try this:

Do a report on pizzas and use this site to print pictures of pizzas for your project.

Highlights:

This site is simply delicious!

See also:

The Popcorn Institute

http://www.neology.com/portfolio/popcorn.cfm

Welcome to the World of Willy Wonka

http://www.wonka.com/Home/wonka_home.html

http://puzzlemaker.school.discovery.com/

Overview:

This site, sponsored by Ferguson Consulting, Inc., gives you the opportunity to create your own puzzles and games. A wide variety of choices is available at this site. For example, click on any of these:

- Mazed Things—Escape from hand-drawn mazes.
- Computer-Generated Mazes—Choose the shape and size of the maze.
- Word Search—Type in your own word list.
- Criss-Cross Puzzle—Enter your own words.
- Letter Tiles—Enter a phrase to be unscrambled.
- Number Blocks—Test your skills in arithmetic and/or algebra.

Try this:

Create a cryptogram for social studies. Test it on your classmates and see if they come up with the correct answer!

Design a computer-generated maze for your school newspaper.

Highlights:

This site can be translated into five languages!

When a new puzzle is submitted to the Puzzlemaker site, your creations are ready within about 20 seconds.

See also:

BrainBashers

http://www.brainbashers.com/

A collection of logic, language and math puzzles can be found here.

Thunk.com

http://www.thunk.com

Overview:

You've probably heard about spies using secret codes to conceal their messages from the enemy. At Thunk.com you too can use cryptology (the scrambling and unscrambling of secret messages) to make your own secret messages to send to friends or to keep personal diaries private! Thunk.com is very simple to use:

1. Type or paste a message into the text box.
2. Click the Scramble button.
3. Copy the secret message into e-mail or a word processing document.

To unscramble a message:

1. Type or paste a scrambled message into the text box.
2. Click the UnScramble button.
3. Copy the unscrambled message into your e-mail or word processing document.

Helpful HINT: Use CTRL and C keys to copy and use CTRL and V keys to paste.

Translate this message:

Ef zrccna qfj lfd dbn cqvb bvcn, lfd jvyy unovevcnyl qrin yfcb fo bntanc ode! (thunk.com)

- -

Try this:	Highlights:	See also:
Go to the *Funnies* section and use the scrambled jokes to practice copying and pasting messages into the unscrambler. While you're at it, laugh at some corny jokes other kids have submitted to Thunk.com.	This site is entertaining and lots of fun!	CIA for Kids http://www.odci.gov/cia/ciakids

Government Goodies

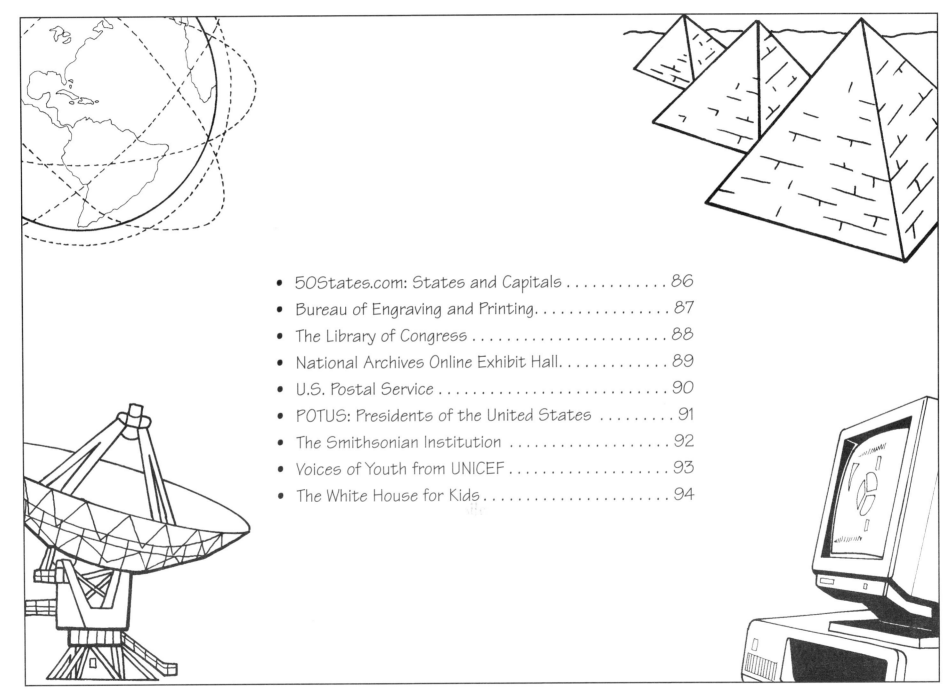

50States.com: States and Capitals

http://www.50states.com

Overview:

Here is the site you've been waiting for! Imagine this: Your social studies teacher has just assigned a report on a state, but all the books you need have been taken out of the library! Stay calm and visit this site. Use the image map and click the link of the state's name to find detailed information for every state in the U.S. Some of the facts at your fingertips are:

- Capital City
- State Bird
- College & Universities
- Constitution Information

- Economy Profile
- State Flag
- State Flower
- Governor

- Maps
- Congressional Representatives
- State Symbols
- Weather

Try this:

Going on a summer vacation? Use this site to gather facts and travel information for your family.

Highlights:

Looking specifically for state songs? Try the *Song* link to avoid other facts.

This site is a gift to every elementary school student.

See also:

Stately Knowledge

http://www.ipl.org/youth/stateknow/

Try the State Capitals and State Flags game for some fun.

Bureau of Engraving and Printing

http://www.moneyfactory.com

Overview:

Have you ever seen a $10,000 bill? Visit The Bureau of Engraving and Printing to see this rare bill and pictures of other paper money online. Go to *The Currency* link and find out whose pictures are on large and small denominations of currency. Then check out *Money Facts & Trivia* where you can find out about the symbolism on money, and view all current currency.

Try this:

Follow the link to the Kids' page and play *Find the New Fifty*, *Face Flips*, and *Count the Cash!*

Highlights:

Lesson links are available for teachers at the Kids' Page.

This is an excellent source for pictures of cash!

See also:

The United States Mint

http://www.usmint.gov

Find coins at this site.

http://lcweb.loc.gov/

Overview:

Welcome to the Library of Congress, one of the most impressive libraries in the world. This Web site, a companion to the resources of the library, offers an amazing number of experiences for the Internet visitor. Some of the possibilities include: *Using the Library* (this includes an online catalog of the collections), *THOMAS* (Congressional Information), the *American Memory* page (America's history in words and pictures), *The Library Today, Exhibitions* (including the American Treasures of the Library of Congress) and much more.

Kids will enjoy checking out some of the online exhibits from the collections, all of which are very large Web sites. Take a tour of some of these amazing exhibitions:

- Frank Lloyd Wright
- The Gettysburg Address
- The African-American Mosaic
- 1492: An Ongoing Voyage
- Scrolls from the Dead Sea
- Rome Reborn
- Women Come to the Front: Journalists
- Temple of Liberty: Building the Capitol for a New Nation

Try this:

Click on *Historical Documents* and browse through the Constitution, the Federalist Papers, or the Declaration of Independence.

Highlights:

This site is packed with photographs, famous documents, stories, books, and government records.

The site map clarifies the overwhelming amount of material to be found here.

See also:

The American Memory Page

http://memory.loc.gov/ammem/amhome.html

National Archives Online Exhibit Hall

http://www.nara.gov/exhall

Overview:

Studying the Declaration of Independence? Come to this site to see this and other original documents of American history online! The National Archives Online Exhibit Hall is the place to find unique primary source materials (original historic documents) for your school projects. Delve into a *Portrait of Black Chicago* and check out prize-winning photographs from the 1970s. Read about a behind-the-scenes meeting between Elvis Presley and President Nixon, or view famous documents like the Constitution, and the Bill of Rights.

A fascinating part of this site is called *Power of Persuasion—Posters from World War II*. At this section you can take a look at images of posters, some of which have become very well known:

- Man the Guns!
- It's a Woman's War Too!
- This is Nazi Brutality
- He's Watching You
- Stamp 'em Out!

Try this:

Print out your favorite poster on a color printer and write a poem to describe the image.

Try reading The Constitution from the original document. Can you read the words?

Highlights:

Take this delightful experience into the archives of the United States and view documents that have made history!

See also:

National Archives and Records Administration

http://www.nara.gov

This is the home page of this site.

U.S. Postal Service Kids' Page

http://www.usps.gov/kids/welcome.htm

Overview:

We all live in the age of telephone and e-mail. It seems natural to pick up the phone to dial a friend or to type a quick note on the computer to send via the Internet. But imagine a time without the telephone and computers. Whether it was a love note or an official government document, letters were the only way to correspond.

Here is a site where you can get to know more about the U.S. Postal Service. Try a game where you can deliver mail in silly ways, play concentration by delivering envelopes into mailboxes, and then answer some questions about the postal system at *Return to Sender*.

- -

Try this:

Ever wonder how subjects for stamps are chosen? Go to *Criteria for Stamp Subject Selection* at *Stamp Information* and find out.

Can't locate a zipcode? It's at your fingertips at *ZIP Code Lookup*.

Highlights:

A wealth of games, puzzles, stamp collecting information, and more can be found here.

See also:

National Postal Museum

http://educate.si.edu/resources/programs/museums/postal.html

http://www.ipl.org/ref/POTUS/

Overview:

Visit this site sponsored by the Internet Public Library that is entirely devoted to Presidents of the United States. Here you will find background information, election results, cabinet members, notable events, and points of interest for every president.

Simply select a president from the list provided, click, and be transported to a world of information. A picture is included for each president, along with information on first ladies and other family members.

- -

Try this:

Do a multimedia report for President's Day and use this site as part of your report.

Highlights:

This site provides accurate and detailed information about presidents along with links to other sources on the Internet.

Alphabetical indexes are provided for names, subjects, and topics in POTUS.

See also:

The American Presidency

http://www.interlink-cafe.com/uspresidents/

Presidents of the United States

http://www.whitehouse.gov/WH/glimpse/presidents/html/presidents.html

Smithsonian Institution

http://www.si.edu

Overview:

It doesn't matter if you can't make it to Washington, D.C. because the whole city is literally at your fingertips at this site. Share the wealth of the Smithsonian Institution, an amazing array of collections, offering a variety of museums and online exhibits. The Smithsonian collects art, artifacts, documents, and treasures, many of which are available online. This is with no doubt one of the highlights of the World Wide Web!

Choose your favorite museum from this partial list, and then sit back, relax, and enjoy the visit. Go to:

- The Cooper-Hewitt Museum
- The Hirshhorn Museum and Sculpture Gardens
- National Air and Space Museum
- Museum of American History

- Museum of Indian History
- National Portrait Gallery
- National Zoo
- National Postal Museum

Added to these museums are at least fifty online exhibits of which a few are listed below.

- Mysterious Manatees
- Ocean Planet
- Spiders
- Women and Flight

- The Jazz Age in Paris
- A Salute to American Musicals
- African American Sacred Music Traditions

For teachers only: This is a great source for education and curriculum materials.

Try this:

Click on any topic from A-Z and find answers to frequently asked questions along with links to other Smithsonian resources.

Highlights:

This site contains more stuff than you could possibly imagine!

Check out *Kids' Castle* and find out about science, animals, sports, astronomy, the arts, and more.

See also:

The Carnegie Museums of Pittsburgh

http://www.clpgh.org/Carnegie.html

Voices of Youth

http://www.unicef.org/voy/

Overview:

Voices of Youth is an attractive and practical site for kids sponsored by UNICEF as part of its fiftieth anniversary celebration. At this site, you can take part in an electronic discussion about the future of children. Discuss ways in which the world can become a place where the rights of every child are protected.

Go to the *Meeting Place* and discuss your views about the following current global issues:

- Children and Work
- The Girl Child
- Children's Rights

- Children and War
- Cities and Children

Try this:

At the Meeting Place, explore the lives of children and their work through stories and photographs. *Take the Child Labor Interactive Quiz and give your opinion about the results.*

Highlights:

This site can be accessed in French, Spanish, and English.

It is packed with valuable information and is designed in a clear, logical sequence.

See also:

Free the Children

http://www.freethechildren.org/

http://www.whitehouse.gov/WH/kids/html/home.html

Overview:

Explore the residence of the President and the first family and read news about what's happening at the White House. Check out the History of the White House or read about kids and pets that have lived in the White House!

Try this:

Take a virtual tour of the White House. You can do this by clicking the *White House History and Tour* link at the main page of the site at:

http://www.whitehouse.gov/index.html

Highlights:

Send an e-mail message to the President and try to convince him to support or not support some current legislation.

See also:

The House of Representatives

http://www.house.gov

History Helpers

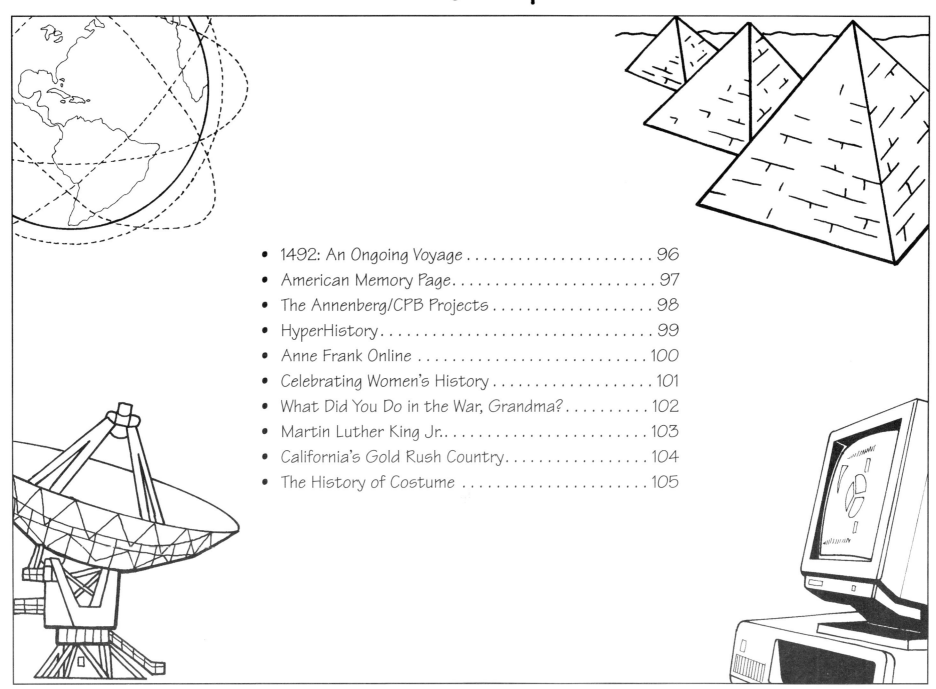

1492: An Ongoing Voyage

http://lcweb.loc.gov/exhibits/1492/intro.html

Overview:

Experience life in 1492, a date which brings to mind one of the most famous explorers in America—Christopher Columbus. This site delves into Columbus' explorations and adventures and the way in which his journeys brought two very diverse worlds, the Mediterranean area and the Americas in contact with each other.

This site addresses many questions, for example, "Who lived in the Americas before 1492?" and "Who followed in the wake of Columbus?"

Take your own journey through this online exhibit and travel through its six sections.

- What Came to Be Called "America"
- The Mediterranean World
- Christopher Columbus: Man and Myth
- Inventing America
- Europe Claims America
- Epilogue

This Web site requires a lot of reading on your part, but it's worth every second!

- -

Try this:

Read about *Christopher Columbus: Man and Myth,* and follow the link to his coat of arms. Then, create your own coat of arms using images from the Heraldry Web site. (See p. 12)

Highlights:

This online exhibit includes images of 22 objects from the original exhibit, including maps and artifacts.

Teachers: This is an excellent addition to an explorers unit.

See also:

First People on SchoolNet: Nations Menu

http://www.schoolnet.ca/autochtone/nations_menu-e.html

Click on *nations* to locate information on specific tribes.

http://memory.loc.gov

Overview:

History comes alive at the American Memory Page! Sponsored by the Library of Congress, this very large site offers over 43 collections of oral histories, maps, papers, videos, and photography. Browse through *California Folk Music* and listen to old-time music. In the Prints and Photographs Division, view *Civil War Photographs*, look through *Baseball Highlights*, check out *Votes for Women*, and learn about the early days of motion pictures (movies), and so much more. This is only a small sample of the over one million items included at this site.

Note: You need the *Real Audio* plug-in, and the capability to play QuickTime, AVI, MPEG and WAV files to fully take advantage of this site.

Try this:

Create a slide show program with images from this site, using *HyperStudio, Kid Pix Studio*, or *ClarisWorks*.

Click on *Today in History* to get a glimpse of notable events from any day of the year.

Highlights:

This is an excellent starting point for researching American history.

A teacher's section is included.

See also:

The History Channel

http://www.historychannel.com

http://www.learner.org/exhibits/

Overview:

Inspired by the Annenberg/CPB video collection, this online companion project offers high-quality multimedia exhibits on the World Wide Web. Educators develop the content for the exhibits along with a team of experts who specialize in Web design and technical applications. This site offers over 35 subject areas that can be used by students, teachers, organizations, and parents. Each month a new exhibit is added to the collection featuring science, art, writing, literature, psychology, geology, and many more.

Some highlights of the collection:

- Cinema—What goes into the making of your favorite movies?
- Collapse— Why do civilizations come to an end?
- Renaissance—Learn about the inspiration of this classical age.
- Middle Ages—Find out what life was really like during this period.
- Russia—What is Russia like now?

Try this:

Go to *Amusement Park Physics* to design your own rollercoaster and see if it passes the safety inspection.

At the *Personality* exhibit, take a personality test to find out how you are perceived by others!!

Highlights:

Each exhibit is packed full of valuable information and is an entire Web site in itself.

Teachers will find valuable classroom information at this site.

See also:

The History Place

http://www.historyplace.com/

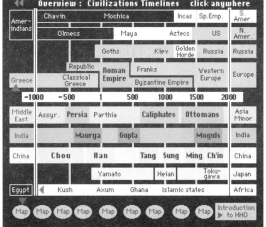

http://www.hyperhistory.com/online_n2/History_n2/a.html

Overview:

Based on a world history chart, HyperHistory covers 3,000 years of people, events, maps, and time periods. Imagine the chart from your history class coming alive, and with a click, all sorts of people and events from the past appear! For example, click on *Events* followed by a click on *1901-1910*. HyperHistory brings up a colorized chart (civilizations are color-coded) with a vast array of entries, including the *Boxer Revolt in China, Henry Ford Founds the Ford Motor Company, J. Barrie Writes Peter Pan, L. Lumiere Develops Color Photography, Congo Becomes a Colony of Belgium,* and many more. There is an incredible amount of information packed in this site that covers 3,000 years!

Try this:

Looking for a map of the Mongol Empire in a hurry? Click the Map button, and you will find it.

Highlights:

There is a huge number of files at this site, but individual pages are able to load quickly.

Updates and additions are continually being made to this page.

See also:

Any Day in History

http://www.scopesys.com/anyday/

Anne Frank Online

http://www.annefrank.com

Overview:

Learn about Anne Frank, a German-Jewish teenager who was forced to go into hiding during the Holocaust. Anne and her family, along with four others, spent 25 months during World War II living in an annex of rooms in Amsterdam. During this period, Anne wrote what was to become one of the most widely-read personal accounts of the Holocaust. This site offers a glimpse into Anne's story through several sections:

- A photoscrapbook of Anne's life and family
- Excerpts from her diary

- A tour of the Annex,
- A brief history of the Holocaust

Try this:

Find locations for the exhibit Anne Frank in the World: 1929-1945, and try to attend the exhibit when it tours your area of the country.

Highlights:

Excellent original archival materials are used at this site.

A section on education is available for teachers.

See also:

A Student's Forum of Art and Poetry About the Holocaust

http://remember.org/imagine/index.html

Celebrating Women's History

http://www.gale.com/freresrc/womenhst/index.htm

Overview:

Come to this site and celebrate the 150th anniversary of the Women's Rights movement. Read about courageous women whose unceasing work to achieve equality for the female half of the American population is still not fully recognized.

Go to the activities section to find a wealth of projects that will add to your understanding of women's history:

- Women's Rulers
- Champions of Women's Health
- Women and War
- Women Volunteers

- Anita Hill: Speaking Out
- Kate Chopin and *The Awakening*
- Mother Teresa
- Communicating Strength

You can go to the time line for key events in women's history, take a quiz on women's history, read excerpts from "Women's Rights on Trial," and find many references on this topic under *Featured Titles*.

Try this:

March has arrived, and you are celebrating Women's History Month in school. Use this site to write a report on a famous woman.

Use the time line information to get ideas and then write a time line about your life!

Highlights:

One of the best parts of this site is the *Biography* section that tells the stories of more than 60 women.

See also:

Biography.com

http://www.biography.com/

Biography Maker

http://www.bham.wednet.edu/bio/biomak2.htm

This site will guide you through writing a biography.

What Did You Do in the War, Grandma?

http://www.stg.brown.edu/projects/WWII_Women/

Overview:

Learn about your grandparents' (and great-grandparents') generation, the years before and during World War II. Young students in the Honors English Program at South Kingstown High School interviewed Rhode Island women from this unique era and then created this site packed with memories and personal interviews. These are examples of some of the interviews:

- Coming to Terms with the Holocaust and Prejudice at Home
- A Pacifist in a Time of War
- A School Teacher Minds the Home Front
- Raising Six Children Alone
- War Sparks a More Active Role for Women

Twenty-six interviews are included as well as a World War II time line, links to oral history resources, articles, bibliography, an audio presentation, and reference pages.

Try this:

Make up a list of questions and interview your grandmother or another senior citizen; find out what she did during WWII.

Highlights:

This is an excellent example of a school Web site.

Teachers can integrate this site into a World War II history unit.

See also:

A People at War: Women Who Served

http://www.nara.gov/exhall/people/women.html

Martin Luther King Jr.

http://www.seattletimes.com/mlk/index.html

Overview:

Get to know Martin Luther King Jr. at this comprehensive site which covers the Civil Rights Movement and the role Dr. King played in the struggle for equal rights. Some of the highlights from this site are listed below:

- a time line of the Civil Rights Movement
- a time line of Dr. King's life
- sound clips taken from Dr. King's speeches

- an interactive quiz on Martin Luther King
- discussions about civil rights among students
- ways to celebrate King's birthday

- -

Try this:

Click on *The Movement* and then *Images of History*. Follow the arrows at this section and take a photographic tour through the national civil rights movement in the Seattle area.

Highlights:

This is a very good site from *The Seattle Times* which takes an in-depth look at the impact of Martin Luther King.

See also:

Black History

http://www.gale.com/freresrc/blkhstry/index.htm

©Leslie A. Kelly

Courtesy Show Me
The Gold® Logo

http://www.goldrush1849.com

Overview:

Strike it rich historically at this comprehensive site which covers the Gold Rush through stories and photographs. Take the virtual tour that begins when James Wilson Marshall discovers gold at Sutter's Mill in 1848. Read *The Way West* which describes the migration of the hundreds of thousands of gold seekers who flocked to California to get rich (the Forty-Niners) and tells about the addition of California as the United States of America's thirty-first state.

Try this:

Do you need a writing project for school? Visit this site and then write a story through the eyes of a forty-niner. For example, include the trials of the journey westward as well as the obsession with becoming rich in California.

Highlights:

A map, extensive photographs, and information illustrate this site.

Related links and books are provided.

See also:

Gold Fever Exhibition at the Oakland Museum

http://www.museumca.org/goldrush.html

THE HISTORY OF COSTUME
By Braun & Schneider   c 1861 1880

http://www.siue.edu/COSTUMES/history.html

Overview:

Imagine this:

You have written a play set in sixteenth century Italy for your English class. The sets, characters, and lines are in place, but you are encountering one serious problem: what did the people wear during that time period?

Your problems are answered at this site which provides pictures of over 500 costumes from antiquity to the end of the nineteenth century. Originally published as individual plates in a German magazine, the plates were later collected and put in book form. While serving the needs of a modern-day student, the Victorian drawing style may seem a bit cumbersome and outdated. Still, this online book is an excellent source for costume designers and for anyone who is interested in fashion.

Try this:

After browsing through the costumes from various time periods, become your own fashion designer and keep a sketchbook with new ideas.

Highlights:

Use the text index as your guide to view the time periods and costumes on this site.

This would be an excellent addition for period-related literature units.

See also:

The Costume Page

http://members.aol.com/nebula5/tcpmake2.html#schools

Favorite Picks

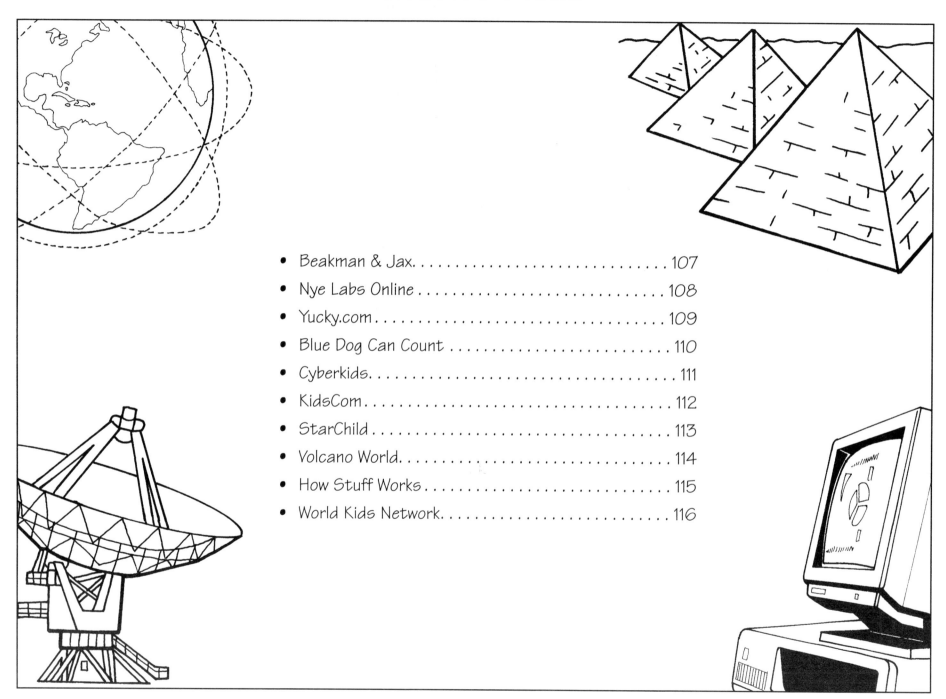

Beakman & Jax

http://www.beakman.com/

Overview:

Visit *You Can* on the Web and stay and play with Beakman and Jax. Click the *Answers to Your Questions* link and find answers to questions like *"How does soap work?"* or *"How does a lever make your stronger?"* Then find out what is coming up in future editions of the TV show or go on a world tour and visit museums with the sets and experiments from Beakman's World.

- -

Try this:

Visit the *Other Tremendous Places to Go* section and find out why feet smell, how mucus protects us, or where Beakman & Jax like to go on the Web.

Highlights:

There is an abundance of funny questions.

If they don't have an answer to your question, simply send an e-mail and check the site in a few days.

See Also:

AskERIC

http://ericir.syr.edu/

Nye Labs Online

http://nyelabs.kcts.org/

Overview:

Did you know that lobsters make noises by rubbing their antennae together or that a computer can add 120,000 numbers in the time it takes a hummingbird to flap its wings? Ask questions from Bill of the TV show at Nye Labs Online and have fun while learning lots of fascinating facts about science! At this site you can check out the *Demo of the Day* and get instructions on how to do experiments that were done in an episode. Click on *Goodies* to hear songs or view photographs and video clips from the show. Go to the *U-Nye-Verse* to find facts about Bill Nye himself, and e-mail Bill Nye your question.

- -

Try this:

Watch an episode of Bill's and then go to the Web site and read the follow-up activity in *Demo of the Day.* Then send an e-mail message with comments about the activity to Bill Nye.

Highlights:

Nye's entertaining approach to science provides hours of science fun!

See also:

Whelmers

http://www.mcrel.org/whelmers/

Find even more outstanding science activities.

http://www.yucky.com/

Overview:

Welcome to the yuckiest, most disgusting, and easily the funniest site on the Internet. First, click on the *Gross/Cool Body* button and find out why you burp, sweat, vomit, have bad breath, zits, pus, and more! Then go to the *Bug World* button and find out everything you always wanted to know about roaches!

Try this:

Go to *Club Yucky* and try out *Yucky Science* or *Edible Science.*

Try creating a *Yucky E-card* and read the poems "Ode to a Worm" and "Worm Hate!"

Highlights:

Kids will be roaring with laughter at this site!

Lots of special effects are included, but they are too gross to be mentioned here. Try them for yourself!

See Also:

The Virtual Body

http://www.medtropolis.com/vbody/

Blue Dog Can Count

http://www.forbesfield.com/bdf.html

Overview:

This simple site is one of the most popular on the Internet. George Rodrigue's Blue Dog performs the arithmetic after numbers are entered in the blank squares. Then, the question is answered by a barking dog! You have the choice of addition, subtraction, multiplication, or division problems.

Try this:

Younger kids can go to this site to practice their math facts.

Test Blue Dog to his limit. If you add 100 + 100, will he bark 200 times?

Highlights:

This is a great beginning site for the younger user. The funny dog and his barking stimulate interest in the World Wide Web.

See also:

George Rodrigue

http://www.bluedogart.com/

Read George Rodrigue's biography and check out some of his other popular paintings.

Cyberkids

http://www.cyberkids.com

Overview:

The goal of this creative site is to create a community of young people from all over the world who share their thoughts and ideas. Take the opportunity to enter contests, tackle puzzles and brain teasers, show off your creativity, read reviews, try magic tricks, find keypals, listen to original musical compositions by kids, and join the Cyberkids Club. (To join the club, you need parental permission if you are under 12.)

Note: *Java* and *Shockwave* required.

- -

Try this:

Register and join the Cyberkids Club (free). You can participate in member activities such as posting messages, chatting, entering contests, submitting drawings, downloading free software, and more!

Highlights:

The Cyberkids *Launchpad* provides interesting spots on the Web to explore. Immerse yourself in art, computers, music, science, nature, museums, entertainment, and all kinds of other activities.

See also:

KidsNews

http://www.kidnews.com/

Kids' writing from practically everywhere is at this site!

KidsCom

http://www.kidscom.com

Overview:

Enter this virtual playground for kids of all ages! Make new friends, find a keypal, travel to other countries, participate in a chat with kids all over the globe (chats are monitored for safety 24 hours a day), play easy or challenging games, and more.

At *Kids Talk About*, you have the opportunity to speak out on a new question every week, write a story with characters provided by KidsCom, or tell the Web community about your favorite pet.

Note: *Java* and *Shockwave* required.

Try this:

Young kids, go to *Mousers*, the section of the site designed for little KidsCom kids!

Offer your opinions to presidents and prime ministers by visiting the *Voice to the World* link.

Highlights:

Parents and teachers can visit their own special section at *ParentsTalk*. Share messages with parents from around the world or check out some activities at Family Fun.

See also:

Kids' Space

http://www.kids-space.org/

StarChild

http://starchild.gsfc.nasa.gov/docs/StarChild/StarChild.html

Overview:

Welcome to StarChild, a learning center for young astronomers put together by a special team at NASA. This site covers everything you'd want to know about the universe and includes many high quality photographic images. Click on The Sun, The Moon, The Planets, The Asteroid Belt, or Comets, and see what you can find.

The *Space Stuff* section is very interesting also and offers information on Astronauts, *Space Travel*, the *Hubble Space Telescope, Space Wardrobe, Space Probes*, and *Who's Who in Space*.

Try this:

Gather information at StarChild for a Science report. Include digital images from this site for your presentation.

Highlights:

An excellent glossary is useful for fact finding.

Printable versions of pages allow for higher quality printouts.

See also:

The Nine Planets

http://www.seds.org/nineplanets/nineplanets/nineplanets.html

Volcano World

http://volcano.und.nodak.edu/

Overview:

Volcano World provides fascinating information about volcanoes, one of the most dramatic phenomena in nature. At *Volcano World* you can experience the excitement of this unique natural wonder through many activities, numerous volcano images, volcano observatories, and even volcano video clips! Enrich your volcanic knowledge with interactive experiments, volcano indices, and by keeping involved with currently erupting volcanoes of the world.

Try this:

Go through the *Kid's Door* and check out *Volcano Art*, take the *Kid Quiz*, go on *Virtual Field Trips* at *Volcano Adventures* and e-mail questions to the *Volcanologist*.

Highlights:

Volcano World enriches learning experiences by delivering high quality images and other data.

See also:

Stromboli Online

http://www.ezinfo.ethz.ch/volcano/strombolihomee.html

Find even more volcano photos, eruptions, maps, drawings, and video clips.

How Stuff Works

http://www.howstuffworks.com

Overview:

Welcome to How Stuff Works, a wonderful place to explore the way things work in your everyday world. Join Marshall Brain, the creator of this site, as he helps you understand just about everything. For example, he answers the following questions:

- How does a VCR work?
- Why does a thermos keep the hot stuff hot and the cold stuff cold?
- How is a 500,000-pound jet able to get off the ground?
- How do Web servers deliver Web pages from anywhere in the world to your computer?
- What makes digital clocks and wristwatches tick?

Mr. Brain has an uncanny ability to communicate complex ideas clearly and has a passion to explain how just about anything works! To prove it, the traffic at this site has peaked to approximately 10,000 users a day!

Try this:

Send your e-mail address to How Stuff Works and receive information about new articles added to the Web site.

Highlights:

If you are searching for something in particular, a full text search facility is available.

This site is designed for both young and old kids!

See also:

The Last Word

http://www.last-word.com/

World Kids Network

http://www.worldkids.net/welcome.htm

Overview:

World Kids Network is a large site dedicated to the advancement of children's education. "Be anyone, do anything, or find out almost anything" is the motto of the site. You can join clubs, play games, do homework, visit museums, or even be a volunteer for the World Kids Network (WKN).

The WKN is a place where kids can explore the world with wonder in a safe and enjoyable environment with tons of new things to experience!

Try an excursion to one of the places below:

- The Marsupial Museum
- Internet Safety
- Channel of Wormholes

- Winnie the Pooh and Friends
- G.I.R.L. (Girls Internationally Writing Letters)
- Keypals Club International

- Atomniverse
- Rainbow Road
- Cast of Characters

Note: *Java* is required at this site.

Try this:

Take a guided tour of *Cosmotown* and visit the *Plastic Pink Flamingo* and the *Wiggly Family.* Then check out the *Cosmotown Mall.* How does this mall compare with the mall in your city?

Highlights:

Since this site has been put together by volunteers, you can offer your suggestions and make original contributions to this inspirational world.

See also:

Wacky Web Tales

http://www.eduplace.com/tales/

Touring the World

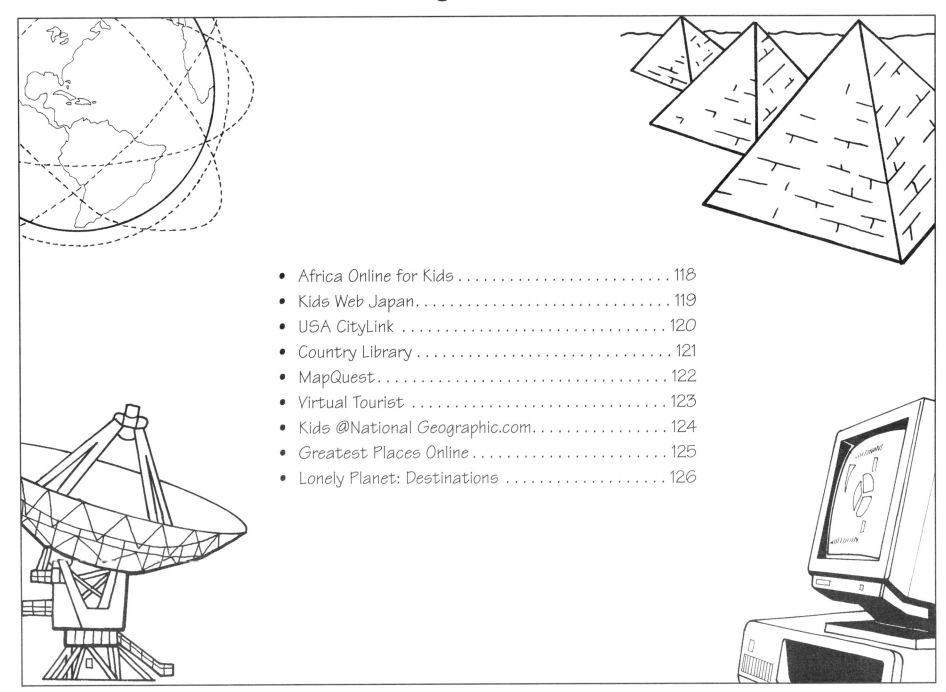

Africa Online for Kids

http://www.africaonline.com/AfricaOnline/coverkids.html

Overview:

Travel to Cote d'Ivoire, Ghana, Kenya, Zimbabwe and a host of other exciting countries in the second largest continent in the world, Africa.

Start at the *Kids Only Zone* and surf through many lands. Then take the online quiz about climate, cities, and names of countries.

A stimulating section to check out is the *Language Page*. Learn about the languages kids speak in Africa—over 1000! Have you heard of some of these languages?

- Arabic
- Berber
- Sudanic
- Setswana
- Teke
- Ubangi
- Cushitic
- Kikuyu
- Malinke
- Kiwahili
- English
- Fula

Give yourself a test and try to match these languages to the countries where they are spoken!

- -

Try this:

Go to *Games & Activities* and try an Africa Word Search, Crossword, or Decode a Message.

Check out the *Sasa Link* (a word in Swahili meaning "Now") and read poems and stories submitted to the site.

Highlights:

Refer to this site for your next report on Africa for social studies.

Lots of information is available here including travel, sports, and news.

See also:

Kids Zone Africa

http://www.afroam.org/children/

Kids Web Japan

http://www.jinjapan.org/kidsweb/

Overview:

Find out what kids are doing in Japan at this informative and colorful site. Read regularly updated news stories, find out what type of "once upon a time stories" Japanese kids grow up listening to, take part in Japan's rich tradition of Ikebana (flower arranging) and Origami (paper folding), assemble a jigsaw puzzle of the map of Japan, or try some recipes that are popular with school kids in Japan.

Note: *Shockwave plug-ins are required at this site.*

Try this:

Check out *What's Cool in Japan* for kids. Have you heard of any of these fads?

Need information for a report? Click on these sections: *History, Regions of Japan, Politics and the Constitution, Daily Life,* and any other link that is interesting!

Highlights:

Have a question? Go to KidsWeb Plaza and submit your question about Japan.

This excellent site is filled with factual and entertaining information.

See also:

Joseph Wu's Origami Page

http://www.origami.vancouver.bc.ca/

This is a wonderful paper-folding resource.

USA CityLink

http://www.usacitylink.com/

Overview:

The USA CityLink project is a comprehensive city and state listing on the Web. At first glance, the site seems quite simple, but it is one of the most visited sites on the Internet today. It provides users with a starting point when accessing information about cities and states. To use this site, simply follow these steps:

1. Select a state.
2. Browse through the cities available in the state.
3. Choose your city.
4. Gather facts about that city.

Try this:

Doing a state or city report? Start your project at this site and go on a virtual tour.

Play a treasure hunt game. Develop a list of items to gather about various cities, and navigate through the city sites to find these secret treasures.

Highlights:

Comprehensive information is provided in an easy-to-follow format.

See also:

Flag Bazaar

http://www.niceeasy.com.au/flags/worldmap.html

Click on a section of the world to find your flag.

Country Library

http://www.tradeport.org/ts/countries/

Overview:

Visit this comprehensive reference site dedicated to providing worldwide facts. This page is your one-stop, perfect spot for locating all the data you need for class assignments. When you arrive at this site, you will realize that this description is no exaggeration; Country Library offers loads of information on any country of the world and will point you to a variety of helpful resources.　Click on a region of the map or on a particular country.　You will find:

- Country Overview
- Background Notes
- Demographics
- Trade Information

This site provides high level-material that is suitable for older kids in middle school and above.

- -

Try this:

Use the Country Search capability and enter keywords to locate the country information you are looking for.

Highlights:

This is a one-stop source for country reports.

Find *Background Notes* from your desk at home without having to wait in long lines at the library!

See also:

Mr. Dowling's Electronic Passport

http://www.mrdowling.com/

MapQuest

http://www.mapquest.com

Overview:

MapQuest is an interactive mapping service that includes two parts. *Find a map* allows you to find a map of any place in the world. Simply select a U.S. or International city, click *GO*, and quickly get a map. *Driving Directions* provides city-to-city maps or personalized maps for the United States, parts of Canada, and Mexico. For a personalized map just type in your starting and destination address, click on *Calculate Directions*, and your map will appear. The directions are clear and simple to follow. To print your map, don't forget to select the print version option.

Before going on your journey, make a stop at this site. Be prepared!

- -

Try this:

Use the *Find a Map* section to do research on the geography of any part of the world.

Before your next vacation, collect all the maps you need from this site!

Highlights:

This service is free, fast, and easily accessible.

Use this site with students to plan a route to travel. Extend this activity by asking students to estimate traveling time and distance per hour.

See also:

How Far is it?

http://www.indo.com/distance/

The US Census calculates the distance between two places.

Virtual Tourist

http://www.virtualtourist.com

Overview:

Are you planning a trip, or do you simply like to travel? At this site the world is at your fingertips! The Virtual Tourist provides an electronic map of the world with a hyperlink at each section. Simply click on the part of the world you would like to visit and find general information and thousands of pictures of places all over the world. Other useful links at the *Tool* section include a currency converter and time zone information.

Try this:

Collect media on any country and design a pamphlet advertising that country.

Play an online geography scavenger hunt.

Highlights:

Information provided is excellent for a country report.

E-mail tourist information offices in different countries for more access to country facts!

See also:

CIA Home Page for Kids

http://www.cia.gov/cia/ciakids/index.html

Kids @National Geographic.com

http://www.nationalgeographic.com/kids/index.html

Overview:

Join National Geographic's site for kids and check out some of the activities provided. Go to the *Cartoon Factory*, visit the *World of Tarantulas*, read *World Online Magazine*, or even go to the *Pen Pal Network*.

Looking for in-depth explorations? Browse through the lengthy site index at the top of the page, and search the archives. A great section for kids is at *Information Central* that provides information on many topics, for example:

- Animals—bats, manatees, gorillas, tigers and more
- Biographies—famous scientists
- Environmental Concerns—acid rain and the rain forest
- Geography—continent facts
- History—the real *Titanic!*
- Phenomena—unexplained subjects of interest

Try this:

Find *Geography Education* in the index and click on *Map Machine.* Explore continent maps, look at flags, and collect world facts at this interesting part of the site.

Highlights:

The site index provides an accessible menu at every page.

Nice photographs and world information are available at this site.

Teacher information is provided.

See also:

National Geographic.com

http://www.nationalgeographic.com/

| Amazon | Greenland | Iguazu | Madagascar | Namib | Okavango | Tibet |

Greatest Places Online

http://www.sci.mus.mn.us/greatestplaces/

Overview:

Explore the Greatest Places Online site sponsored by the Science Museum of Minnesota and visit the Amazon, Greenland, Madagascar, Namibia, Okavango, and Tibet. Created as a companion to the *Greatest Places* film, this site features colorful tours through these remote areas, interesting activities from the various countries, a travel journal of Namibia, and a chance to get to know the animals from the Amazon to Tibet.

Try this:

Go to the *Making Stickers* section. Follow the recipe for mixing your own sticker glue and then print out a Greatest Place sticker and use the glue for placing it on your bedroom wall.

Highlights:

Hands-on activities give you the opportunity to try engaging projects and games that kids do in some of these great places.

Global systems information is provided and could be used as part of a geography unit by teachers.

See also:

Let's Go Around the World

http://www.ccph.com/

©LonelyPlanet

Lonely Planet: Destinations

http://www.lonelyplanet.com/dest

Do you dream about traveling around the globe from country to country? At this site, your fantasy becomes reality. Start at *Destinations* and use the scroll-down menu to choose a region and then a country. You will instantly be transported to your ideal travel spot and will find photographs, history, attractions, maps, a slide show, facts at a glance, events, and a variety of relevant country topics.

There are neat things to do at this site. For example, click on *Optic Nerve*, and find photographs of almost any country.   Go to *Postcards* and read mail which fellow travelers have sent to the site!

Try this:

Use this site to design a travel guide for your favorite country. Include maps, photographs, and historical information.

Highlights:

Easy and quick navigation through this site makes travelling a breeze!

Other travel links are included at subWWWay!

See also:

World Safari

http://www.supersurf.com

From Neutrons to Numbers

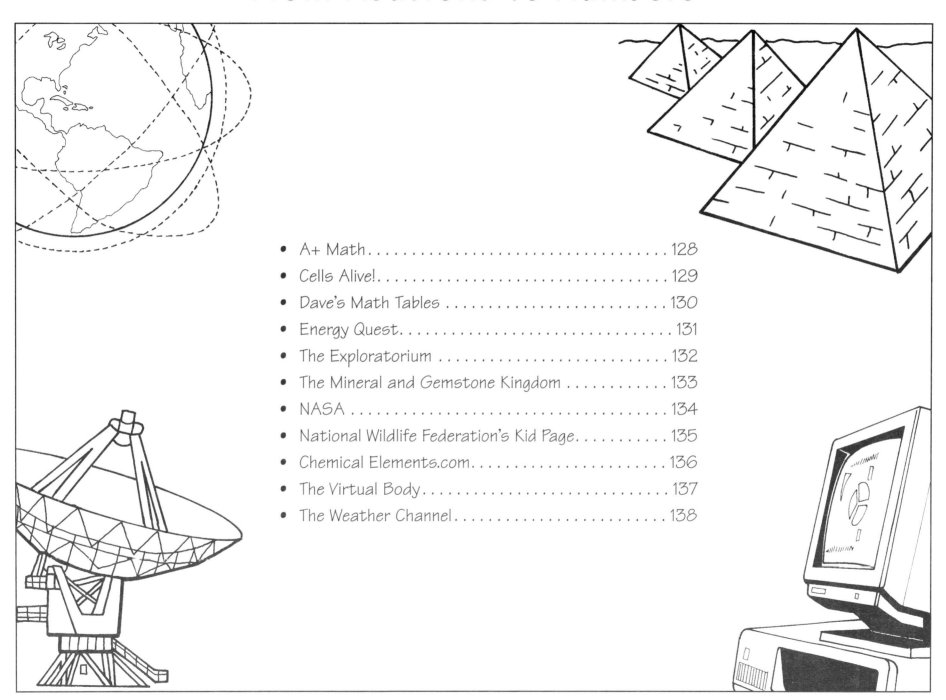

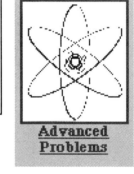

http://www.aplusmath.com

Overview:

Go to this site when you are working on your math skills and want a little extra help. Simple and colorful graphics make learning math lots of fun, especially when you play games like *Matho*, a combination of *Bingo* and math, *Hidden Pictures* and *Concentration*, or use a wide variety of flash cards.

A valuable feature is the interactive *Homework Helper* that allows you to input a problem and your answer. Then it will figure out if your solution is correct without giving you the answer! Try problems in addition, subtraction, multiplication, division, or division with remainders.

Try this:

Challenge yourself and work on problems in the advanced section.

Highlights:

This is a useful site for elementary and middle school students working on their basic skills.

Flash cards are generated quickly and are provided for many topics.

See also:

MEGA Mathematics

http://www.c3.lanl.gov/mega-math/welcome.html

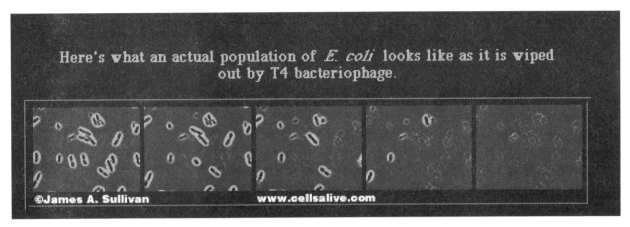

Here's what an actual population of *E. coli* looks like as it is wiped out by T4 bacteriophage.

©James A. Sullivan   www.cellsalive.com

http://www.cellsalive.com/

Overview:

Visit this awesome site that brings biology to life! It is packed full of graphics showing different types of cells in motion. Start with *Penicillin* and watch the video clip of its battle with bacteria. Next, check out *Making Antibodies*, *Parasites* (especially gross-looking things!), and *Dividing Bacteria*. Finally, click on *Pumping Myocytes* and get close to a beating heart.

Try this:

Have you ever gotten a splinter in your finger? To watch a splinter in action, go to *OUCH!* and see how immune cells work in your body.

Highlights:

Kids love this site because of its video clips and animations used to illustrate each subject.

See also:

The MAD Scientist Network

http://www.madsci.org

cup = 8 fluid ounces = (1/2) pint = (1/4) quart = (1/16) gallon
mile = 63360 inches = 5280 feet = 1760 yards
yard = 36 inches = 3 feet = (1/1760) mile
foot = 12 inches = (1/3) yard = (1/5280) mile
pint = 16 fluid ounces = (1/2) quart = (1/8) gallon
inch = 2.54 centimeters = (1/12) foot = (1/36) yard
liter = 1000 centimeters³ = 1 decimeter³ = (1/1000) meter³

Roman Numerals

I=1	V=5	X=10	L=50	C=100	D=500	M=1 000
	$\overline{V}$=5 000	$\overline{X}$=10 000	$\overline{L}$=50 000	$\overline{C}$ = 100 000	$\overline{D}$=500 000	$\overline{M}$=1 000 000

mile = 1760 yards = 5280 feet
yard = 3 feet = 36 inches
foot = 12 inches
inch = 2.54 centimeters

Dave's Math Tables

http://www.sisWeb.com/math/tables.htm

Overview:

Kids, this site will be a valuable resource for you when you are trying to solve a particular problem and can't find the correct formula. At first glance, it may seem as though this site is for older students. But if you look at the tables under the General Math heading, you will find useful materials for your math needs. Some tables you can find are listed below:

- Addition Table
- Number Notation Table
- Roman Numeral Table
- Number Base Systems

- Multiplication Table
- Fraction to Decimal Conversion Table
- Conversion to the Metric system
- Volume Relationship

Try this:

Have a math question? Post your question on this site's Math Message Board for math talk, questions, and answers. There are sections for elementary math through calculus.

Highlights:

Much of this material is suitable for printing.

Conversion utilities are also included at this site.

See also:

The Math Forum

http://forum.swarthmore.edu/

http://energy.ca.gov/education/

Overview:

Learn about energy conservation and environmental issues at this comprehensive site filled with information for both the novice and the seasoned science buff. Created by the California Energy Commission, this site will lure kids into entertaining games, activities, and projects, all packed with science facts.

A few of the site's features include:

- The Energy Story—Go from fossil fuels and solar energy to ocean thermal energy conversion and biomass energy.
- Science Projects—Create a lemon-powered battery or find out how much energy is in a single peanut.
- WATT's That?—Join an entertaining energy game show.
- Percy's Puzzles—Play games, and solve puzzles and riddles.
- Poor Richard's Energy Almanac—Find important energy facts.

Try this:

Get involved in the *Energy Patrol* and find out ways to monitor electricity in your classroom.

Click on *Kid's Tips* and find out what you can do in your daily life to conserve energy.

Highlights:

Energy Quest provides students and teachers with lessons, ideas, and inspiration.

All activities and projects are available in varying degrees of difficulty.

See also:

EnviroLink

http://www.envirolink.org/

The Atoms Family

http://www.miamisci.org/af/sln/index.html

About Us — Online Store — Programs — Visit the Museum

www.exploratorium.edu

the museum of science, art, and human perception

http://www.exploratorium.edu/

Overview:

This incredibly large and impressive site was originally developed as a guide for The Exploratorium Museum in San Francisco. It has branched out to include digital representations of experiments that are performed in the actual museum. Online exhibits include brainteasers featuring *Changing Illusions, Disappearing Act, Depth Spinner,* and others.

Don't forget to drop by the Learning Studio and browse through the following sections:

- Cool Sites at the Exploratorium
- Online Exhibits
- Science Explorer
- Science Snackbook Series
- Cow's Eye Dissection
- Light Walk
- Past Exhibits
- Webcasts

FADING DOT
IF YOU STARE AT THIS DOT FOR A FEW MOMENTS IT DISAPPEARS.

Some of these experiments are quite amazing! This site is not to be missed!

Try this:

Go to *Online Exhibits* and click on *Shimmer.* Your eye movements cause this design to shimmer. Click on *Fading Dot*—if you stare at this dot for a few moments, it disappears.

Highlights:

Check out *Changing Illusions* and tease your brain.

The Science Snack section has ideas for creating your own miniature versions of some of the most popular exhibits at the Exploratorium.

See also:

Franklin Museum of Science

http://sln.fi.edu

THE MINERAL AND GEMSTONE KINGDOM

http://www.minerals.net

Overview:

At this sparkling gem of a site, dig into the world of minerals and gemstones. Find comprehensive information at *Minerals A–Z* and search for a mineral alphabetically or according to a variety of groupings.

Once locating your ruby, diamond, sapphire, or other gem, be transported to a page of information with everything you'd possibly want to know about a stone. Find the following information:

- Color
- Hardness
- Luster
- Chemical Composition

- Uses
- Varieties
- False Names
- Similar Gemstones

The pictures included of Gems and Minerals are absolutely fabulous. Many of the shots can be enlarged, providing a clear view of each stone.

- -

Try this:

Click on *Gallery* and spend some time viewing the beautiful photographs available in the online Image Gallery.

Highlights:

All materials are arranged with an easy-to-use interface.

Content is for both amateurs and experts.

See also:

The Mineral Gallery

http://mineral.galleries.com

NASA

http://www.nasa.gov

Overview:

Enter the National Aeronautics and Space Administration (NASA) home page and be prepared to browse through another mega-site. Even visitors who want to remain earthbound will be impressed with its wealth of resources. Look through video and audio clips to gain a fuller understanding of NASA's advancements in aerospace. Enjoy reviews of space missions, visits to various space centers, the question and answer section, daily NASA news updates, and a variety of NASA projects.

This site may feel like an endless black hole of space facts, but it is best to take your time, be patient, and return for future space missions.

Try this:

Use the Search Tool to find NASA Astronaut Biographies and then write a report on an astronaut.

Go to the *Multimedia Gallery* and browse through NASA's still images at the *Photo Gallery*.

Highlights:

To get a handle on this large site, use one of the two search options. First, there is the NASA Subject Index, which is organized WWW information by subject. Second, you can search the NASA web by entering keywords in the search box.

Check out these related NASA sites!

SpaceLink

　http://spacelink.nasa.gov

SeaWiFs Project—including the Jason Project

　http://seawifs.gsfc.nasa.gov

The NASA K–12 Internet Initiative Page

　http://quest.arc.nasa.gov

National Wildlife Federation's Kid Page

http://www.nwf.org/nwf/kids/

Overview:

Learn about nature with the National Wildlife Federation. Go on a *Cool Tour* by following animal tracks through *Water, Wetlands, Endangered Species,* or *Our Public Lands.* Then check out articles in English and Spanish from *Ranger Rick,* the environmental magazine for children. Click on *Games* and then check out the list below:

- Mad Libs
- Mix'em
- Match'em
- Quiz Yourself
- Rick's Riddle Picks
- Did you know?

A favorite game is Match'em where you identify animal tracks by clicking on the pictures of animal paws. Do you know what pig prints look like? pigeon feet? Ever seen turtle prints? Good luck!

Try this:

Did you ever think about helping the Earth but didn't know where to start? Click on *You Can Help the Earth* and learn about how to become an Earthsaver or about how to start an Earthsavers group.

Highlights:

Check out Ranger Rick's *Homework Help* and find information about *Wildlife,* the *Environment, Math, Science,* a *Big Library* and a *PANIC BUTTON!*

See also:

National Wildlife Federation

http://www.nwf.org/

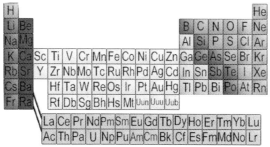

Chemical Elements.com

http://www.chemicalelements.com/

Overview:

Studying chemistry this year? Then you must check out this exceptional site. Yinon Bentor created this site as an eighth grade science project several years ago. Since then, this page has evolved to become an excellent source of information as well as a fine example of a truly interactive Periodic Table.

Using this chart is simple. Simply click on any element, and a page of basic information will pop up with almost everything you'd want to know about any element:

- Name
- Symbol
- Atomic Number
- Atomic Mass

- Melting Point
- Boiling Point
- Number of Protons/Electrons

- Number of Neutrons
- Classification
- Crystal Structure

Try this:

Click on *Help* and find explanations for words like symbol, mass, atomic number, melting point, and more.

Try viewing the Periodic Table in different ways. To do this, use the links found under the "Show Table With" menu heading.

Highlights:

Working on atomic structure as part of a homework assignment? Go to this site for help and look at in-depth diagrams showing electron distribution, energy levels, protons, and neutrons.

See also:

Web Elements

http://www.webelements.com/

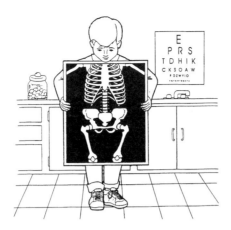

The Virtual Body

http://www.medtropolis.com/vbody

Overview:

Come to The Virtual Body, an absolutely amazing site! Experience an interactive and animated tour of the brain, digestive system, heart, and skeleton. Roll your mouse over a graphic of the human heart, and the name of the anatomical part along with a description of its function appears! Watch the heart pump blood as you adjust the heart rate slider to control blood flow. Then listen to a narrated tour. This is quite fascinating!

Don't forget to check out the *Human Brain, Human Skeleton* and *Digestive System* sections, which provide equally exciting graphics and information.

Note: *Shockwave* plug-ins required at this site.

Try this:

At the *Human Skeleton* section, drag bones from a pile and build your own skeleton.

Check out the Brain Book and find out what foods give neurons (brain cells) the most nourishment.

Highlights:

Teachers: Use a projection device in your classroom and display this site as an exciting addition to an anatomy unit.

See also:

Human Anatomy Online

http://www.innerbody.com/

The Weather Channel

http://www.weather.com

Overview:

Weather affects everyone. It offers daily variety and combines elements of prediction, anticipation, and surprise. The influences of weather are everywhere and make a difference in your day-to-day school activities. At the Weather Channel, take the opportunity to become more involved with weather. Telecommunications provide the opportunity to track events, manipulate data, and gather and compare real life-information.

Some handy features of this site follow:

- A pull-down menu allows you to find weather information on over 1,700 cities/countries.
- Weather maps have current conditions, US Doppler radar, and a U.S. Satellite Picture.
- A weather glossary is handy.
- A Storm Encyclopedia provides preparation for a storm.
- Disaster safety tips are available.
- You have the option of customizing your own weather home page.

- -

Try this:

Locate the city where you live at Weather.com and find a five-day weather forecast. Print the forecast and then compare the daily predictions with the actual weather.

Highlights:

The *Teacher's Lounge,* found on the Education page, provides extraordinary resources for teaching and learning about weather phenomena.

See also:

Intellicast

http://www.intellicast.com

EarthWatch Weather on Demand

http://www.earthwatch.com/

Kiddie Korner

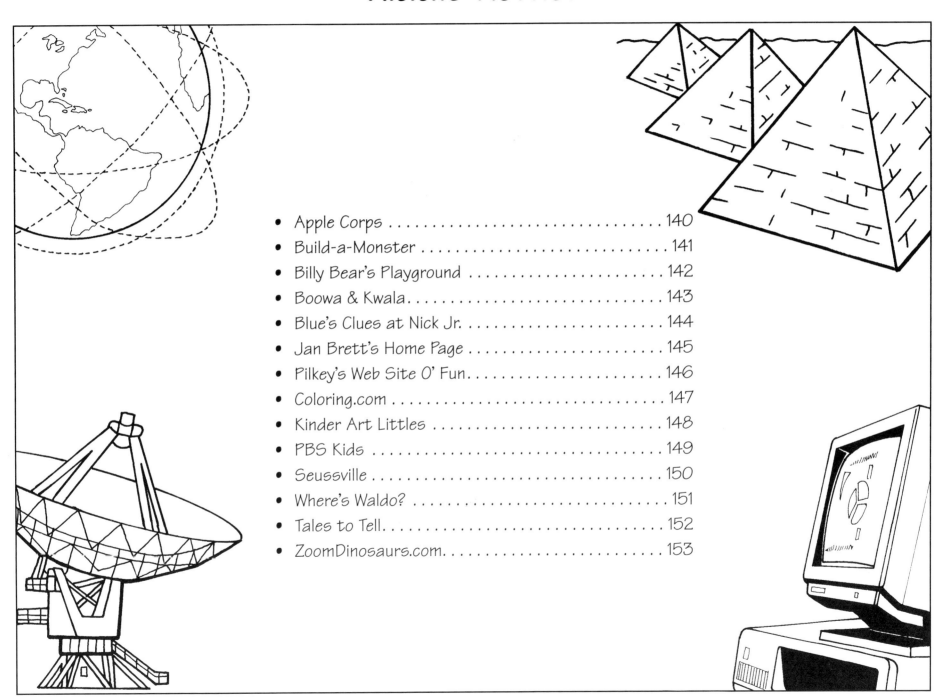

http://apple-corps.westnet.com/apple_corps.2.html

Overview:

Create faces on fruit and vegetables at this irresistible site based on the popular Mr. Potato Head by Hasbro. At Apple Corps, however, you are not limited to potatoes only. This site provides the opportunity to design faces on a variety of fruits or vegetables.

Directions:

1. Select the fruit or vegetable you wish to design by clicking on *Change Vegetable.*
2. Click on a button next to a facial feature.
3. To place your piece on the face, click on the vegetable itself.
4. Repeat the process until your silly face is completed.
5. Laugh a lot!

Try this:

Print and save images of your creations to develop an Apple Corps Art Gallery!

Highlights:

This site offers great graphics and is easy to play.

This is a good starting point for a younger Internet user.

See also:

Mr. Edible Starchy Tuber Head

http://winnie.acsu.buffalo.edu/potatoe/

http://www.rahul.net/renoir/monster

Overview:

Visit this simple yet entertaining site and have fun creating your own animals and monsters. Creatures have three sections from which to choose: a head, torso, and legs. It is your job to decide which animal you wish to use for each of these parts of the monster, whether it is a frog, bird, dinosaur, or wacky creature. Then you simply click on the head, torso, and legs of your choice and, magically, a new monster is created.

This is a great activity for the young Internet user who can click and create while combining the parts in a variety of ways!

Try this:

After you create several creatures, print the pictures and brainstorm names for your characters.

Highlights:

This site uses CGI scripting and works fine with slow modems.

This simple activity provides great entertainment for young children.

See also:

Build-a-Rocket

http://www.rahul.net/renoir/rocket/

http://www.billybear4kids.com/

Overview:

Come to Billy Bear's Playground and join in the fun with thousands of other Internet users. This colorful and graphically packed site is so popular that sometimes 5,000 people visit in only one hour!

It's practically impossible to go through the entire site in only one visit, so take the opportunity to return to this page time and time again. In fact it may be helpful to browse through one section a visit. Some sections to try are listed below:

- Clipart
- Animal Scoops
- Fun & Games
- Holidays
- Post Office
- Story Books
- Show & Tell

A very popular feature of this site is the holiday portion. Visit Billy Bear on almost any holiday (New Year's, Valentine's Day, St. Patrick's, Easter, Pesach, Mother's Day, Father's Day, Fourth of July, Halloween, Thanksgiving, Christmas, Hanukkah, Kwanzaa, and birthdays. Also find holiday games, holiday downloads, print & play activities, crafts, e-cards, and online coloring pages!

Try this:

Use Billy Bear's *Clip art* to create your own picture book.

Print personalized animal stationery of kangaroos, kaolas, lions and a host of other creatures at *Animal Scoop*.

Highlights:

Need birthday party help? Go to *Holidays* and find balloons to color, a personalized birthday certificate, birthday stationery, and game ideas for your upcoming event!

Graphics, colors, activities—that's what you'll find here.

See also:

Rebus Rhymes: Mother Goose and Others

http://www.EnchantedLearning.com/ Rhymes.html

There is one Rebus Rhyme for every letter of the alphabet. This is very rewarding for beginning readers.

http://www.boowakwala.com/

Overview:

Travel around the world in a hot air balloon with Boowa and Kwala. Each month these cute critters take you to a new country in their search for Kwala's family. Click on the arrows, and at each new destination they will teach you a song and offer interactive games to play. This highly graphic site uses Flash and has lots of animations, sounds, and music.

Note: Some loading time is required, but even that can be fun at this site! Shockwave plug-ins are required.

- -

Try this:

At *Games Galore*, go to the *Land of Hats*. Mix and match the hats, faces, and bodies.

Highlights:

Find colors, animations and songs extraordinaire!

The site is available in French and English.

See also:

Theodore Tugboat Online Activity Centre

http://www.cochran.com/theodore/

©Nickelodeon. Used by Permission.

Blue's Clues at Nick Jr.

http://www.nickjr.com/bluesclues/home.tin

Overview:

At Blue's Clues, a play-along program for preschoolers, figure out the problem of the episode by observing Blue's paw prints. Download pictures, go to *Blue's Boutique*, and check out Extended Learning Activities. Young kids will enjoy this playful site filled with colorful sights and sounds.

Other Nick Jr. characters found on this site:

- Little Beat
- Allegra
- Gullah Gullah
- Franklin
- Eureka

Try this:

Go to *Recipes* for Extended Play and learn to make a newspaper hat.

Go to *Blue's Shockwave Game Collection* and play the game of the week.

Highlights:

Great graphics, games, and fun can be found here.

Additional information for teachers is available.

See also:

Webtime Stories

http://www.kn.pacbell.com/wired/webtime/

Welcome to Jan Brett's Home Page

© 1999 Jan Brett

http://www.janbrett.com/index.html

Overview:

The Hat, The Mitten, Armadillo Rodeo—these are some of the beloved books written and illustrated by Jan Brett. At this site you can view pictures of Hedgie, the rabbit, the goose, and her other famous cast of characters. With a color printer, you can print your very own life-size masks of these loveable animals and put on a play for your friends and parents. Some other activities available at this site:-

- Fun projects you can make
- Coloring Pages
- Piggybacks for Teachers
- Hedge-a-Gram
- Send a Postcard
- Books by Jan Brett

If you know a teacher or librarian, Jan has a special teacher's pack available for free. Just write her at the address listed on this Web site.

Try this:

Click on *Activities*, and then on *Fun Projects You Can Make.* Select *Learn to Draw an Armadillo.* Follow Jan Brett's directions and create your very own armadillo!

Do you enjoy baking? Try the Hedgehog Cookie recipe for a rainy-day treat.

Highlights:

Send an e-mail letter to Jan Brett, and she'll write back with a monthly Hedge-a-Gram.

This site is exceptionally colorful and attractive and is quick to load.

See also:

Children's Storybooks Online

http://www.magickeys.com/books/index.html

http://www.pilkey.com/

Overview:

Remember the Dumb Bunnies? Just in case you don't remember who they are, Dav Pilkey is the author of these hysterically funny characters. To continue with this author's sense of humor, indulge in his site and choose from a wealth of possibilities, including the all-time favorite, Dav's Page O' Fun.

Click on *Fun 'N Games* and paint a coloring-book page, using the "watercolor" paints. Wander over to *Print 'N Play* for *Tuffer Stuffer,* a place loaded with searches, mazes, and connect-the-dots games; or read about The Adventures of Captain Underpants on the Flip-O-Rama. These are just a few samples of what can be found at this playful Pilkey page.

Try this:

Go to *How 2 Draw* and follow drawing instructions for a Dumb Bunny.

At *Fold 'N Fly* follow instructions for folding a "Pilkey-Powered Paper Pilot Pug Plane"!

Highlights:

The activity level at this site ranges from preschool to early elementary.

Boring Teacher Stuff is included!

See also:

Story Hour at the Internet Public Library

http://www.ipl.org/youth/StoryHour/

http://www.coloring.com/

Overview:

Coloring.com is a favorite site for young Internet users with a very simple and easy-to-use interface. First, choose a drawing from the following categories:

- Easter
- Other Stuff
- Football
- Halloween
- Thanksgiving
- Animals
- Birthdays

Then follow these directions:

1. Click on the title of a picture.
2. The picture will appear along with a palette of colors.
3. Click on a color.
4. Indicate where you want the color by clicking on a particular section of the template.
5. The page will reload quickly.
6. Repeat the process until the picture is complete!

Try this:

E-mail your colorful creation to a friend or relative.

Experiment with complementary and contrasting colors.

Highlights:

This site provides an excellent way for little ones to become comfortable moving a mouse and creating online!

New colors and templates are constantly being updated!

See also:

Crayola

http://www.crayola.com

http://www.kinderart.com/littles.htm

Overview:

This site is packed with art projects and ideas especially created for little hands. The *Activities* section includes a wide assortment of free art ideas to bring out that creative spark in every special kid. For some unusual and interesting ideas, go to *Aquarium in a Bag, Baggie Paint, Boo-tiful Trees, Feet Treat, Fun with Wallpaper, Glue-In, and Potato People.* Then click on the following sections for more fun:

- Art and Craft Recipes—Find simple recipes at the art kitchen.
- Kindercolor—Print original pages to color.
- The Bookstore—Arts, crafts, and cooking are found here.
- The Fridge—Art is submitted by kids.

Try this:

Go to the KinderArt Kitchen and follow the recipe for scented paint. Then use the paint to make a picture of fruit. What a pleasant smelling picture!

Highlights:

These simple yet creative activities are suitable for classrooms or indoor play.

See also:

Idea Box: Early Childhood Education & Activity Resources

http://www.theideabox.com/

Aunt Annie's Crafts

http://www.auntannie.com/

©Public Broadcasting Service

PBS Kids

http://www.pbs.org/kids

Overview:

This Web site is a great entrance into the many pages found on PBS; it features all your favorite characters and friends. Begin your journey at PBS kids Online and then launch into other home pages for Arthur, Barney, Mr. Rogers' Neighborhood, Storytime, Theodore Tugboat, Charlie Horse, and others. Each TV site offers activities, coloring pages, and games, along with the high quality-entertainment you'd expect from public television. With thousands of pages to explore, you'll have loads of learning fun.

Try this:

Forgot the words to a Mr. Rogers song? Learn the words at his song archive.

Browse through Keno's list of favorite-favorite books and choose a few that you'd like to borrow from the library on your next visit!

Highlights:

Click on *Pre-School* to find activities designed for thc youngest PS kids. Find animals, reading, music, science and friends!

Teachers: Check out the PBS TeacherSource for classroom resources.

See also:

Children's Television Workshop

http://www.ctw.org/

Seussville

http://www.randomhouse.com/seussville/

Overview:

Meet Sam-I-Am, Yertle, Horton and the Whos, the Cat in the Hat, the Lorax, and all your favorite Dr. Seuss characters at this site. Delve into this zany world and play fun-filled games, prepare tasty recipes, color funny pictures, and enter the trivia contest each month. Kids, you will really enjoy the game link that provides hours of entertainment with its silly list of choices:

- Hooray for Diffendoofer Day! Game
- Sylvester Mcbean's Sneetch Belly Game
- Elephant Ball
- The Lorax's Save the Trees

- The Cat's Concentration Game
- Green Eggs and Ham Picture Scramble
- Horton's Who Hunt

And if all this isn't enough, take a detour to *More Fun* for other surprises!

Note: All games require *Shockwave*.

- -

Try this:

Check out printable games like *Connect the Dots, The Cat in the Hat, What did Marco See?, The Cat's Hat Maze,* and more.

Highlights:

Enjoy delightful fun in a typically Seuss-fashion!

See also:

The Arthur Page

http://www.pbs.org/wgbh/arthur/

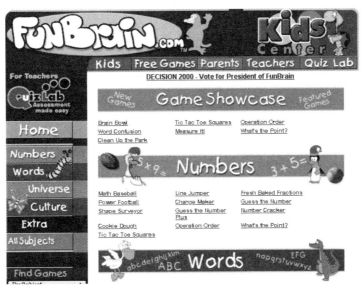

FunBrain.com
http://www.funbrain.com/kidscenter.html

Overview:

This is an excellent site full of wonderful learning games. Children have many choices when they select a game to play, by age, difficulty level, or subject and grade level. Results are posted immediately after the game is completed. You will find games in the following links:

- Numbers
- Words
- Universe
- Culture
- Brain Bowl

Try this:

Check out one game in each of the above links. Choose a different difficulty level for each game.

Highlights:

These games are really cool:
Number Cracker in Numbers.
What's the Word in Words.
Where Is That? in Universe.
Piano Player in Culture.
Kid vs Parent in Brain Bowl.

See also:

Duck Hunt

http://www.ee.duke.edu/~js/ducks.html

Look for the teeny-tiny duck in the pictures.

Tales to Tell

http://www.thekids.com

Overview:

Tales to Tell offers delightful picture stories from around the world. Rhymes, fables, animal stories, adventures, folk and fairy tales, all with beautifully illustrated pictures, are yours to read and explore. Browse through the list of stories in the following four sections:

- Rhymes & Nonsens
- Fables & Animal Stories
- Stories from Everywhere,
- Heroes & Adventure

After choosing a section, click on a story you'd like to read or ask a grown-up to read it to you. You'll find familiar stories like *The Seven Voyages of Sinbad the Sailor*, and *The Straw Ox*, or you'll find stories with unusual names like *Osoon Turkey*!

Try this:

Go to *Kid Stuff*, click on *Sound Off*, and read stories submitted by kids. Then write your own story, submit it to *Tales to Tell*, and have your very own moment in the literary spotlight!

Highlights:

High-quality links are provided at *Best of the Net*.

If you enjoy stories from long ago and faraway, this site is for you!

See also:

Carol Hurst's children's Literature Site

http://www.carolhurst.com

152

ZoomDinosaurs.com

http://www.EnchantedLearning.com/subjects/dinosaurs/index.html

Overview:

Zoom Dinosaurs is great for any dinosaur enthusiast! At this site you can navigate through masses of well-organized information, including *Dino News, Dinosaur Fossils, Dinosaur Quizzes,* and even an illustrated *Dinosaur Dictionary* with over 500 entries!

Check out *Dinosaur Fun* and try games, puzzles, quizzes, and even vote for your favorite dinosaur!

Try this:

Click on *Dinosaur Jokes* and then tell the jokes to your friends.

Go to *Games, Puzzles, and Quizzes & Activities,* and try the *Scrambled Dinosaur* activity or try *Match the Dino Skull to the Dinosaur* activity!

Highlights:

This site has an easy interface and is packed with delightful dinosaur activities!

Dinosaur information sheets are fabulous references for writing a dinosaur report. Check it out!

See Also:

The Children's Museum of Indianapolis

http://www.childrensmuseum.org/kinetosaur/e.html

Basic Terminology

Bookmark	An electronic marker to a Web page
Browser	Software which allows users to access and browse the World Wide Web (*Netscape Communicator* and *Microsoft Internet Explorer* are examples of browsers.)
Download	The process of retrieving a file from a remote server and transferring it to your computer
E-mail	(electronic mail) A system of sending and retrieving messages from one computer to another
Home Page	Main or introductory page of a Web site
HTTP	(HyperText Transfer Protocol) Coding language used to create hypertext documents on the World Wide Web
HTML	(HyperText Mark up Language) The language used to format Web documents
Hyperlink	(link) A hypertext link or connector which can be in text or graphic form (Clicking on these highlighted words or graphics will transport you to another item.)
Image map	A graphic on a page that contains hyperlinks
Internet	A global network of computers that allows millions of users to exchange and share information.
Net	A short form for the Internet.
Plug-in	An application that allows a graphic browser to complete a task or to view a specific file. (Use plug-ins to view 3-D images, see animations, or listen to audio files. Many games require *Shockwave* and/or *Java*.)
URL	(Uniform Resource Locator) The address or location of a document available on the Internet
Web	A short way to say World Wide Web (WWW)
World Wide Web	(WWW) A part of the Internet system containing hypertext documents that allow for point and click navigation
Web site	A collection of Web pages on the World Wide Web centered around a particular theme

Web Site Collections

These following sites were developed as collections of resources on the Web. Use them to find information on a variety of topics.

B. J. Pinchbeck's Homework Helper

http://school.discovery.com/students/homeworkhelp/bjpinchbeck/

B.J. and his dad started this site to create homework resources on the Web.

Berit's Best Sites for Children

http://www.beritsbest.com/

This is a directory of safe sites for children up to age 12. Sites are rated and listed by subject.

Carol Hurst's Children's Literature Site

http://www.carolhurst.com/

Hurst's site offers a collection of book reviews, books, activities and professional ideas for teachers.

Cool Sites for Kids

http://www.ala.org/alsc/children_links.html

The American Library Association collected and reviewed this list of sites.

The Electronic Zoo

http://netvet.wustl.edu/e-zoo.htm

An extensive list of animal resources is found here.

G.R.A.D.E.S. Archive

http://www.connectedteacher.com/library/search.asp

Classroom Connect handpicks quality education sites.

Kathy Schrock's Guide for Educators

http://school.discovery.com/schrockguide/

Schrock's categorized list of Internet sites useful for teachers and students is quite well-known.

Mega Homework Help Page

http://www.maurine.com/student.htm

Hundreds of good homework sites are found here.

Safesurf Kid's Wave

http://www.safesurf.com/kids.htm

A list of SafeSurf approved sites as organized by category.

Sites for Parents and Caregivers

http://www.ala.org/alsc/parents.links.html

This is another ALA list of excellent recommendations.

700+ Great Sites

http://www.ala.org/parentspage/greatsites/

These are "amazing, spectacular, and mysterious" Web sites for kids from the ALA.

Zoo Links

http://www.ala-net.com/zoos.html

This is an alphabetical list of zoos around the nation.

Favorite Museums Online

Art Institute of Chicago
http://www.artic.edu/

The British Museum
http://www.thebritishmuseum.ac.uk/

The Carnegie Museums of Pittsburgh
http://www.clpgh.org/Carnegie.html

The Metropolitan Museum of Art
http://www.metmuseum.org/

The Louvre
http://www.louvre.fr/

The Montreal Museum of Fine Arts
http://www.mmfa.qc.ca/a-sommaire.html

Smithsonian Institution
http://www.si.edu/

WWW Virtual Libray: Museums Around the World
http://www.icom.org/vlmp/world.html

The Uffizi Gallery in Florence
http://www.mega.it/eng/egui/monu/ufu.htm

Index of Web Sites